TAMING THE WOLF
Full Moon Meditations

By Steve Hounsome

TAMING THE WOLF
Full Moon Meditations

ISBN 1 898307 37 7

Cover design and illustration by Daryth Bastin

Published by:

Capall Bann Publishing
Freshfields
Chieveley
Berks
RG16 8TF

Acknowledgements

I would like to thank all those who have given me support in writing this book, especially to Carrie, without whose love and strength it would not have emerged. Also to all meditation students, past, present and future, who knowingly or unknowingly, have helped simply by being there to listen, share and occasionally, howl. Also, my thanks to Julia and Jon, for allowing a dream to come true.

My grateful thanks to Tracey Havril for her inventive Tarot pictures and to Carrie for the Chakra picture.

To the memory of my Mother, who in her own silent and subtle way, was the catalyst for it all.

And to the Wolf within me.

About the author

Steve Hounsome is a teacher of Meditation in the Winchester and Southampton areas of England, and views his work as spiritual service. He has qualifications in Healing, Psychic Studies and the Tarot. He has also studied Meditation, Natural Magic, the Qabalah and the Western Mystery Tradition extensively. He is also a professional Tarot consultant and is a founder member and Secretary of the Professional Tarot Society. He uses the Tarot as a therapeutic tool, for complete development of Body, Mind and Spirit. He was born in Brighton and now lives in Winchester with his wife, dog, cat, rabbit, two guinea-pigs and a rat.

CONTENTS

DEDICATION

I want to run then sit and cry
'Neath shady Moon and wonder Why
Knees drawn close, a shadow by
A rippled pool, silhouette of tree
You, solitude, Mother and me.

Taken by your patient pull
Attune my soul with you when Full
Illuminating one and all
Partaking of the breath of life
Opens the gate to the afterlife.

The howl of wolf so full of pain
The bay of dog not seen again
Silver waves once pulled from rain
Comforting light, enduring night
Of Lovers and Fools, guiding their plight.

Nightmares, visions, Goddess aloft
Terrible beauty, pale and soft
Beckons me on, seek secrets lost
The sacrifice and endless hours
The miracle of intuition flowers.

FOREWORD

There are many thousands of gatherings all over the world in which people meet to celebrate the Moon being 'full'. These celebrations take many different forms. Some meditate, some dance, some enact ritual. All are valid and effective and all profoundly affect those involved. The word celebration is used deliberately, for the Full Moon has, since pre-Christian times, been seen as a time of blessing, when the mysterious and powerful Goddess turned her face and her blessing, upon the dwellers of the Earth.

The Moon, as Goddess, has been venerated and worshipped for thousands of years, its importance paramount in the minds of those who lived a life very different to our own. To these so called 'primitive' peoples, the planets and heavenly bodies that could be seen in the night sky were more than just dead lumps of matter floating somewhere above them. They were the abode of the deities that had a direct and vital effect on their everyday lives: the success of the harvest, the coming of the rains, the guiding light through the dark night. With this importance came then the personification of these planets, stars, Sun and Moon into gods and goddesses. The movements in the heavens visible from below were seen as depicting the lives and actions of the deities. It was therefore vital that these powerful and not all together placid beings were appeased and worshipped correctly, so as to bestow blessings and abundance upon the devotees. There was then a close, even intimate relationship between these deities and the followers, which it may surprise you to know, can still be achieved today.

Even in the midst of our automated, scientific world that moves along at a pace many find difficult to keep up with, we can still find communication with the Old Ones. This may involve seeking out the wild and lonely places where they still live, and in the case of the Full Moon, sitting bathed in its glow, your eyes never leaving the shadows that play strangely around you in the half light. Then, just as you begin to feel fear reaching out its icy fingers, the Goddess smiles down at you and rewards your patience. From behind the clouds appears a glowing globe, seemingly close by, whispering words of comfort and inspiration to you.

Thus begins the communication with this most ancient and mysterious of deities. To give yourself to the Moon and the Goddess in this way awakens feelings that are deep beyond words. The use of the term celebration, becomes clear only to those who have felt the breath of the Goddess upon them and danced in the moonlight at the dead of night. They have heard the howl of the wolf and responded, unable to resist the urge from within, from the very centre of their being. To see and feel the Goddess acknowledge and bless you in this way, at the height of her powers, is to instigate an automatic response that is the celebration.

Through this book we shall explore and experience some of the ways in which humanity has seen fit to celebrate the time of the Full Moon. We will see just what happens when we meditate with the Full Moon. It is my deepest hope that this will inspire you to join this celebration and experience for yourself the exhilaration and peace that comes from living a life that follows, by instinct, the cycles of Mother Nature. We shall explore those cycles, as they apply to the Moon and look at the rich and varied History and Mythology associated with it. This will give us a deeper understanding of the purpose behind the many gatherings taking place these days. We will see how the shift into the much publicised 'New Age' is more than just the latest commercial trend. We will see how the phases of the Moon affect us and learn not to become the plaything of these forces. Rather we can learn how to move in tune and time with them, utilising these powerful influences for the good of ourselves, the Earth and the whole Universe.

We will see also the need for us to come to know and befriend that part of us that we do not know and may fear. Symbolised as the wild wolf, we can together tame this animal and emerge with a faithful friend, loving us unconditionally simply because we are there. First we must encounter the wolf in his lair and meet this wild force on his own ground. Together then let us join the merry band of seekers devotedly celebrating the time of the Full Moon in spiritual service. Let us join hands and together throw back our heads and howl.

1
THE MAGICIAN

1. Who's Afraid of the Big Bad Wolf?

Wolves have had a long association with the Moon, not all of it pleasant or comfortable. The traditional symbolism of the wolf howling at the Moon is of the forces of the unconscious mind being unleashed. In this Chapter we will look at this symbolism and discover why this is so and what we can do about it. We will take a look at the history and mythology of the wolf in order to discover why the wolf is portrayed as such a threat and just why wolves howl at the Moon. We will discover through this that the wild wolf has its counterpart within us. Just as the wolf has become tamed with its successor, the family dog, so do we need to tame this wild, unknown part of ourselves. One way that we can do this is to align ourselves with the phases and movement of the Moon through the year. First however, we must look at what this dark part of the human system is.

Psychologists will tell us that the unknown is the contents of the unconscious mind, that which we do not wish to know or refuse to acknowledge due to painful memories or emotional traumas. This may have its roots in many things, from childhood memories through to past lives. As a general rule, what we do not know about ourselves, we fear. Courage is needed on the path as we explore these dark and hidden areas. It is rather like taking a walk in the countryside at night, away from the neon glow of the city. It is then our minds and eyes play tricks upon us and we feel all sorts of irrational fears rising from within. It is easy to imagine that you see people and 'things' amongst the shadows, with only the moonlight to guide you.

We need then to rationalise those fears and to face those deeper parts of our minds and selves, if we are to find a deeper peace and rest within. The moonlight, and the Moon itself, then becomes our friend and ally, a pleasant light in the darkness, familiar and comfortable. The terrors of the night recede and we can go on our way, with no fear of what lurks in the physical and mental shadows.

It is a common image in films that plays upon these irrational but understandable fears. The lone walker stumbling across the moor, mist swirling about them. In the distance a long and eerie howl is heard, and the camera pans upwards to reveal that the Moon is Full, surely the worst omen yet. The wolf is unseen, yet is feared, like the hidden depths of our minds. If we only took a little courage in hand we may find that the wolf is curious and easily frightened itself. We begin to see the frightened child within ourselves, not the ravaging beast we once thought. This means we must tame the wolf within by facing those hidden depths. How we do this may vary, but as we shall see, the process and regular practice of celebrating the time of the Full Moon, is one such method. This is however only a part of the reason for such a celebration. It is almost an unwanted but welcome side-effect, as we shall see.

Wolves then, have been portrayed as evil creatures, to be feared and hunted, often by those denizens of Hollywood. Recently we have seen a refreshing glimpse of a truer nature of the wolf in the film 'Dances with Wolves'. Here the animal is portrayed as timid and curious, venturing near human contact only when it is absolutely sure there is no threat. We witness its instant disappearance several times when unknown strangers appear. Once tamed however, it remains a loyal and helpful friend, until going the way of many wolves in real life. Such is the fear of wolves that two animals introduced to North America to study their behaviour were shot by over-zealous huntsmen in the 1970's. Only two centuries ago, wolves that were caught were burnt at the stake.

It is clear that as a race, humanity is fearful of the wolf and so of itself. Even in the language we use today there are clues as to the fears we have about wolves. The phrase 'to hold a wolf by the ears' is to be in a desperate situation. To 'cry wolf' is to give false alarm, to be a lone wolf is to be a mysterious, unknown stranger. Then we have the 'wolf in sheeps clothing', the evil lurking beneath the innocent disguise. Lastly, a great many people in these times have to fight to 'keep the wolf from the door', fending off starvation and desolation.

Even in the fairy stories we tell our children and grow up on ourselves, the wolf is portrayed as a threatening, often evil character. The story of Little Red Riding Hood is well known, where the wolf lurks in the wood waiting to prey on the innocent girl. He finds his way to her, through her granny, symbol of wisdom in the story. Red Riding Hood, in her innocence, does not realise that the place of her granny has been taken by the wolf. Thus the wolf acquires wisdom and assumed the role of the teacher, which has since become his role in animal lore and symbolism today. In the story of the Three Little Pigs, the wolf is again the threat. Often the wolf appears in this guise of a moral teacher, with a lesson to show us. By observing these lessons we thus befriend and tame the wolf and live safely on. The wolf has become the mentor.

Continuing the allegory we have made with the wolf and our unconscious minds, we can see that once we tame this creature, we gain a companion for the rest of our days, to whom we can turn for guidance and help at any moment and who never complains or refuses us. There is a sacrifice we must make in order to win this friendship, which we will come to in due course, but this really is a small price to pay for the rewards one gains. Remember we are dealing here with only one level of Full Moon Meditation, that of the psychological relationship. The spiritual aspects and the wonderful relationship we can establish with the Goddess of the Moon is still to be explained and experienced. It is this that is perhaps the real reason for Full Moon celebration.

For now, let us return to our new friend and a short examination of the mythological beliefs concerning wolves. The wolf acquires its evil image from many different races and cultures across the world. In the Persian tradition of Zoroastrianism, where the twin forces of good and evil continually battle it out, the wolf is the "wicked two-legged one" - the symbol of evil in human nature. In the book of Jeremiah in the *Old Testament* the wolf is described as "ravaging" and symbolises dishonest gain in Ezekiel "like wolves tearing their prey". In the *New Testament* the false prophets are compared with "ravening wolves". Wolves are also associated with the dead in mythology, as the Egyptian God Upuaut was depicted with the head of the wolf. He was known as the 'Opener of the Way' and was the guide of the dead. The wolf was sacred to Ares, Greek god of war and its worse aspects personified. The Roman god of war also counted the wolf among the animals sacred to it.

Another Roman deity connected with the wolf as a sacred creature was Silvanus, often identified with the older Greek god, Pan, god of wild places and the spirit found in the moonlit forest. Pan was feared as the inducer of terror or 'Pan-ic' to those in high and lonely places, where perhaps the howl of a wolf might echo. Scaring folk in this way was great fun to Pan, suggesting that he may not have been as evil as first thought. It is possible to think that if we face and accept Pan as a deity of the wild places, seeking to befriend the forces found there, we may also make a friend of the wolf, who will come to us obedient and faithful as a dog.

There are suggestions of a more beneficent side to wolf worship and belief and it is from here we begin to see the wild and tame sides to the wolf, and thus to ourselves. In Japan, the wolf is admired for its ferocity and determination in attack. It is regarded as coming from heaven and is therefore to be worshipped, offering protection against the evil bear. The cult of Zeus Lycaeus in Greece would sacrifice and eat a wolf so as to absorb its essence, suggesting there was something of benefit they wished to gain from the wolf. The story of Romulus and Remus is well known from Roman folklore, these twins being suckled by a wolf at the founding of Rome. This depicts a different and altogether more pleasant side to the wolf. This is echoed in the book of Isaiah where the wolf is symbolised as feeding with the lamb to represent the coming new Heaven and Earth. Yet even here the wolf is the image of Satan, a theme reflected in mediaeval literature.

The Norse myths have the wolf as the bringer of victory, ridden by Odin, the god of battles. The wolf is also Fenris, the incarnation of evil and one of the monsters created by Loki, his mother. The god Tyr lost a hand in the attempt to chain Fenris, a reminder here that to tame the wolf is not to chain and suppress, but to know and befriend him. To the Norsemen, the wolf was one of the three traditional beasts of battle, along with the raven and the eagle. In Norse mythology, two wolves pursue the Sun and the Moon across the sky, ready to devour them and bring about the destruction of the world. The three female helpers to the Norse gods of war, the Valkyries, rode on their terrible way, taking the dead to Valhalla, the Otherworld, on wolves.

The races with the strongest feelings for wolves are perhaps the two that have had the clearest bearing on our beliefs concerning these animals today, the North American Indians and the Celts. Together these peoples see the wolf not so much as a threat and a killer, but have seen the advantages of it and tamed it, at least, or perhaps at most, in spirit.

To the Plains Indians of America, the wolf was noted for the attributes of endurance and for being a fast runner. Thus the scouts of the Oglala Sioux would wear a wolf hide, so as to give themselves these properties. The howl of the wolf was thought to have special powers, it being noted for being more musical in tone than most animal sounds. Even this however, has negative connotations, as a wolf-note' is to sound a discordant or 'bum' note in music. These wolf songs were taught to the Sioux in dreams and visions. We can then tie in the music of the wolf and its associations with the Moon with the belief of the Moon being the Goddess that inspires poetry and creativity. Perhaps it is this that the wolf expresses when he howls so enchantingly at the night sky, expressing his alienation from this force and his desire to connect with it.

A creation story of the Seneca Indians of the north-eastern United States has a different explanation for this. It is their belief that the Wolf Spirit sang the moon up into the sky, causing all wolves today to howl in recognition and remembrance of this.

The Nookta Indians of the area around Vancouver Island had the wolf as one of their totem animals. This meant to those adopting the wolf in this way that they must take part in a ritual that symbolised their death and subsequent rebirth, this time with the power and essence of the animal with them. The individual would live for a period of one year outside of the clan, after having been carried into the woods by wolf-men, wearing wolf skins and headdresses and symbolically slain. He would then be readmitted, having been resurrected and born anew, into his new life, with the wolf.

To the Indians the period before the arrival of Spring was known as the wolf-month, a month being of course a complete lunar cycle. Wolves live in mountainous and forest areas, as well as in the tundra of the Arctic. For this reason they are seen as teacher and guides, knowing their territory and where they might find food and shelter. The land being sacred to the Indians, the wolf was thus seen as a teacher of sacred things, bringing new ideas, and transformative psychic energies. This of course gives us another link with the Moon, being popularly thought of as the force behind psychic energy and power. The original home of these teachers, the old gods and goddesses, was regarded as Sirius, also known as the dog-star and the brightest star in our sky.

So we can see that coming to understand and correctly channel these psychic energies, is to move with the power and therefore the phases of the Moon. This is then, to symbolically change the unknown wild power, the wolf, to the known and tamed companionship of the dog. There is evidence to suggest that dogs have been domesticated since the times of ancient Egypt and have since offered companionship and unswerving devotion to humanity, also allowing themselves to be used for guarding and herding.

Now let us turn to the beliefs and associations regarding wolves with the ancient and fiery peoples of these islands, the Celts. These date back to at least 2500 B.C., in the British islands, after the movement of Stone Age agriculturalists from North Africa. The wolf was prevelant in the Celtic lands of Wales until the 15th century and Ireland and Scotland until the early 18th century and was the longest surviving large predator in Britain. Now however, the wolf is extinct in these lands and in many others where it once flourished.

Strong Celtic beliefs regarding the wolf gave it a place of prime importance in their culture. To these people, the growth and successful harvest of crops such as corn, was vital not just to a plentiful supply through the long winter months, but the very difference between life and death. Much significance was therefore placed upon the goddess of the land and the spirit of the corn itself. The Celts named this corn goddess Cerridwen, whose name means 'white grain' and was also known as the 'old white one'. When harvesting the corn, the spirit was said to retreat into other necks of the crop, until it had been chased into the very last one. The person who cut this last ear of corn was known as 'The Wolf'. They then took on the persona of a wolf, and must bite the lady of the houses they visited. They were eventually placated and 'tamed' by being presented with a large piece of meat. This satisfied the wolf and the threat was removed. This belief of the wolf as the spirit of the corn was echoed in sayings in France and Germany. When the wind made the crops sway, it was said "the wolf is in the corn".

One of the chief deities for the Celts was known as Cernunnos, a horned god in the image of a stag. His influence is still felt today, as he survives in the wild places left to us, as the lord of the wild woods, bearing many similarities to Pan. His horns are those pictured in many Scottish dances when the arms are raised above the head. Cernunnos was often pictured holding a wolf on either side, to demonstrate his mastery and lordship over the animals, thus another instance of taming the wolf. The market cross at Kells near Dublin bears this picture.

The Irish goddess of fertility and healing Brigid, whom we shall learn more of later, pictured as the Christian St Brigit, is also shown in the company of a wolf. The Morrigan, a triple aspected war goddess and a figure much feared by the Celts, once attacked the great war hero, Cuchulainn in the guise of a wolf, but without success. Indeed the wolf was said to win every battle, no matter who the victor, feeding on the bodies of the dead. The wolf finds its way into the Arthurian stories through the magician Merlin, having a wolf as his companion during his spell of living as a hermit in the forests.

Thus the wolf came to have a principle place in the culture and life of the Celts, becoming ingrained into the structure of their society. This is demonstrated partly through the Welsh tale of Math. Upon learning that his nephews Gwydyon and Gilvaethwy had raped the virgin lady Goewin in his own bed, Math set out to seek compensation on her behalf. He turned the two into deers, pigs and wolves each for a year, so that they might each bear a child by the other. The wolf cub that was produced was baptised by Math in his human form, thereby taming him, and named Bleiddwn, 'Bleidd' meaning wolf. Variations of this have since been common in Welsh personal names.

One of Ireland's great Kings, Cormac, was taken by a wolf bitch while his mother slept and suckled by it. Cormac was found, became King and subsequently took a band of wolves with him wherever he went, which at least to some degree, must have been tame.

Robert Graves tells us in '*The White Goddess*', the source that finds its way into so many magical book bibliographies (this now being no exception!), that because wolves howl at the Moon, feed on flesh, live in wooded mountains and their eyes shine in the dark, they have been associated with the Moon and the Goddess since ancient times. Certainly the surprise meeting of a howling wolf in the dead of night, its eyes gleaming yellow and mouth drooling over a bleeding corpse, is enough to strike terror into even the stoutest of hearts.

But perhaps there is something deeper that links the wolf to the Moon and gives us our fear of this animal. Historical research shows that only once has a wolf attacked a human, other than attacks by rabid animals. This was between the years of 1764 and 1767, in central France. Two wolves are reckoned to have killed approximately 100 people, mostly children who were herding their flocks. These particular wolves had mated (which wolves do for life) and one was with cubs. Their markings were abnormal and it is thought that they were the first generation of the wolf-dog cross breed and so unstable. This is unique in the history of the wolf species.

It is supposedly a well-known fact that wolves howl at the Moon, their mournful sound echoing around our minds. Why? Animal behaviourists tell us that this is for territorial reasons. Wolf packs have a definite territory, with an area that is 'no wolf's land'. This is scented and a wolf, upon smelling another wolf's scent will howl so as to alert the other pack as to its presence. The reason it does this is to avoid a confrontation it may well wish to avoid. Wolves can be fierce and threatening animals, but not to humans, as we have seen. Shepherds in the areas of Northern Europe where wolves once existed but sadly are no more, used only to carry a stout crook, to wave and so frighten any wolf that may approach them. The wolf can and will however, attack whole flocks of sheep and other livestock, making many a kill in one night.

A wolf straying on to another packs' territory then, is in danger of being attacked. On smelling the other packs' scent it responds to this with fear, and howls. This alerts the neighbouring pack to its presence and the howl is instantaneously answered by a chorus of equally harrowing howls. If one wolf howls, the whole pack howls. Animal behaviourists tell us that it is virtually impossible for a wolf, on hearing a howl, to resist the urge it feels within to howl itself.

There is then an instinctive and primeval urge in the wolf to express itself in this way. There is also a certain something at this instinctive level that links the wolf pack together to become one. With all the pack, heads back and howling for all they are worth, there is a unity that goes beyond any conscious understanding or explanation. It is as if they have become entranced by the Moon above them and together they take up the call.

We must now return to another of the inhabitants of magical book bibliographies, Carl Jung. This Swiss psychologist expounded the theory of the collective unconscious, a level of the human mind at which we experience certain phenomena, reactions and instincts not individually, but together, as a species. It is this that makes the use of symbolism, in such forms as the Tarot, each card being a collection of appropriate symbols, such a powerful tool for self-development and counselling, when used to its fullest extent. So we have certain symbols that in their antiquity and power, humanity the world over reacts to and interprets as one. The image of the wolf baying at the Moon with its mournful howl is one such symbol. As we have seen its symbolism is that of the release of the unconscious forces of the mind. If we can experience these forces collectively, through Jungs 'collective unconscious', it follows that we can utilise and 'tame' them collectively. This is then, the same instinct in wolves that causes the pack to howl in unison.

One of the means by which we can do this is to gather at the time when those forces are at their greatest and we are at out most receptive. This is the time of the Full Moon, when since ancient times there have been gatherings all over the world to celebrate with song, dance, ritual, enactment and meditation. By a process of deep attunement to these unconscious forces emanating from the Moon while in its 'full' phase, we can discover a communication and relationship to hitherto unknown depths within ourselves. Where once we would have retreated with fear we can tread sensitively and with love to find a deeper fulfilment from within. Just as the Moon relates to these unconscious forces, so by welcoming and harnessing this power, collectively and individually, can we come to know the source of our fears and instead find love and acceptance. This love, compassion and understanding can then be turned into a potent force of itself, that can be used, by way of spiritual service, to help others on their path and for the 'healing of the wastelands' - the healing of our planet, which is now so vital a task.

This collective means of working is a different process to the individual path we all have that is the search for enlightenment, depicted for instance, in the 'Seekers Quest' of the Tarot. This is the journey of the Fool through each of the 22 stages or cards of the Major Arcana that constitute the 'trumps' of the Tarot deck. Those familiar with the Tarot will immediately recognise the relevance of one such card to our studies here. Card 18 is The Moon. This shows a Full, round Moon above a pool of water, out of which a crayfish or lobster crawls towards a dog and a wolf, both of whom are entranced by the Moon, often shown howling.

Taking only one part of the meaning of this card, it graphically illustrates for us the necessity for taming the wolf and for moving with the force of the Moon. The dog and the wolf have both allowed themselves to become hypnotised by the Moon, their wild instincts getting the better of them. Unbeknownst to them, the crayfish, symbol of the depths of the unconscious with all its fears, crawls out of the pool to claim them. Instead of letting the Moon control us with its mysteries and its constantly moving and changing influences, we must learn to move with these tides and act accordingly. This leads us to face those fears as we have seen, and so progress.

18
THE MOON

Another aspect of the interpretation allotted to this card comes from the absence of any human figure in it. From this we can draw a parallel with their being an absence of identity, or familiarity with the truth of ourselves as we really are. Under the half-light of the moon our sense of familiarity and identity is apt to go and we are left only able to trust out intuition, as we struggle to distinguish reality from illusion. We must trust that our intuitive self will guide us through this dark night. We emerge, in the next card, into the full light of day, as it is The Sun, but we cannot appreciate the full, simple reality of this until we have experienced the animalistic 'dark night of the soul' that is the experience of The Moon card.

We can see in the card the path that leads into the future, lit by the Moon. To accurately follow this path we must trust our intuition. Each person must then come to know what their intuition is in each moment. It is this intuition that enables the moonlight to be a guiding rather than blinding light. By aligning ourselves with the phases of the Moon and the changing influences She has upon us through the year, we can adapt to these natural cycles and experience for ourselves, first individually then collectively, the miracle of intuition. In this way, the wild wolf within becomes the dog: intuitive, curious, loyal and a valued and loving friend. We in turn, become more loving, intuitive and, you will find, loyal to the Goddess of the Moon, who bestows these gifts and to whom we must now introduce ourselves.

2. THE GODDESS AND THE MOON

Just as we have seen the many and varied connections of the wolf with fear and the Moon, so there are many gods and goddesses, from various pantheons that give us the instinctive yet mysterious link we feel with that silver globe in our night sky. It is perhaps worth mentioning here that it is at least in part from the lives and stories of these Old Ones that we get the ingrained beliefs we have. These mythological tales spark a recognition in us of something primitive and deep. Their stories are the story of the human psyche and its development and so we are able to learn from beliefs and cultures the world over that have adopted these myths as their own. Each has something to offer and each tells us, in the case of deities associated with the Moon, something of our instinctive and primeval link with the Goddess. Through a short introduction to some of the chief deities of the Moon, we shall introduce ourselves to the Lady of the Moon and in this way, establish our own personal link and feeling for her. We will find that she is not some long lost, imaginary being with vengeful tendencies and unapproachable aura. Rather, if we are sincere and polite, she will present herself to us, offering her blessing to each in her own way.

To the peoples of ancient times, their gods and goddesses were not beings who looked on humanity as a plaything, but those that directly shaped their lives and their very survival. These people came to know, not believe, in their gods, as beings with characters and personalities. Many of the rituals and celebrations they carried out in their names depicted aspects of their lives and characters. In this way they came to familiarise themselves with the very essence of their gods. They felt their presence within and so could communicate directly with them, to establish and follow their wishes. Today, there are those who still feel and know the gods in this way, through ritual and meditation. Through dedication and a genuine desire to know them, they come to know their gods personally, each individual gaining a real and deep love for the deities they worship and uphold. We too can know these beings for ourselves and here we can meet, worship and communicate with the deities of the Moon, following that which you feel the strongest link with, in your heart.

Each one must come to the altar of the god or goddess he feels drawn to and must request their presence, with a beating heart and with patience. Though we shall see here the gods and goddesses associated with the Moon from different races across the world, and so realise that they can be worshipped in many different ways, as different characters, it is as well to remember that 'all the gods are one god' and that at some level they conjoin. That level for us is the Moon itself, as that which orbits the Earth. This is our central symbol, to which we attach ourselves and here give godly form and thought. Let us travel then across the world and introduce ourselves to the many aspects of the deities of the Moon, approaching with respect and sincerity.

Much has been written of how the lost land of Atlantis contained temples, some to the Sun and others to the Moon, including works by the respected occultist and author Dion Fortune. For an age the worship of these deities fulfilled the people until baser human traits caused the infamous downfall. It is thought possible that the magicians and priests of Atlantis were aware of their coming demise and so sent out teachers to different parts of the world to establish mystery schools based on their knowledge. Some of these teachers are said to have found their way to the lands of Egypt, as well as to our own British shores. The teachings they brought with them were used to establish the worship of their own deities, the devotees being careful they did not fall into the same traps as their Atlantean counterparts. These teachings have survived in some form, and it is said that with the coming 'New Age' further information will be discovered to add to what we know. So it may be that what we practise today also contains a distant echo of that original, fabled land and its power.

The Moon has even been connected as having a part in the downfall of Atlantis. It is possible that this was caused by a shift in the Earths' axis, resulting in a change in the position of the Moon in relation to the Earth. This in turn affected the tides of the Earth, the resulting flood being that which caused the destruction of Atlantis. It is well known today that the Moon affects the tides and affects a pull on all waters. It has been said the Moon may not have been visible in its present form from the Earth in Atlantean times, there being a layer of vapour mist around our planet. With the shift in its position, so the view of the night sky from the Earth changed. If the Moon became visible then, or its visibility drastically changed, is it possible that she could have been seen as the cause of the catastrophe? Imagine the effect of seeing a new planet in the sky and knowing of the great changes to come to the planet, as the Atlanteans did. It is easy to suppose that this heavenly body would be both revered and feared. Is this then the cause behind the mystery of the Moon and the fear of its power that as we have already seen, affects us deeply.

This is merely my own fanciful thinking, but it may be that we have here traces of the origin of Moon worship as a mysterious being capable of great effects. Today we have a rather different view of the Moon, having come to understand scientifically just how it pulls the waters of the Earth. Yet as all those who have walked by its light and sat wondering beneath a clear night sky will know, the Moon still retains its mystery and instills a little of its fear. We may have conquered its matter, but perhaps we are still to come to know its mystery within us. By aligning ourselves with its movement through the year and its different phases in our calender, we can come to reveal that mystery, which each one who comes must do for themselves. Thus the Goddess that is the Moon becomes a friend rather than foe.

The Egyptians are thought then to have inherited some of the practices and perhaps beliefs of the Atlanteans, though making rather more of a success of them since their civilisation did not meet the same end as their predecessors. At this time the Moon was thought of as a male god rather than female goddess. Somewhere in the midst of the various and sometimes complex mythological beliefs of our ancestors, the view and influence of the Moon has changed from masculine to feminine. Thus today we have the view of the Earth as female, the Sun being the potent masculine force with its penetrating rays to fertilise the body of the Earth and make the crops grow. Where then does that leave the role of the Moon in this vital play of creativity itself? As we shall see, 'She' has a role of extreme importance, as if she has been directing the path and development of humanity from behind the scenes all along.

To the Egyptians the Moon was first Khons and then later Thoth. Khons was depicted as having the lunar circle round his head with the crescent shape attached. He was a god of healing and was viewed as a type of guardian angel for the King. Interestingly, he was known as 'The Counsellor', indicating something of the role the moon can take when we become familiar with it. Thoth began with his time on Earth as a god of magic and became overseer of the Moon on his departure. He was responsible for measuring time. Immediately then, we link healing and magic with the Moon, both of which feature prominently in our meditations, as we shall discover. The link between the Moon and the passage of time is shown through the story of Thoth and the so-called 'epagomenal' days. In this tale, the lunar god Thoth, also being god of mathematics and science played a game of draughts with the Moon. In this he won a seventy-second share of her light and power and since one seventy-second of 360, the number of days then in the year, is five, Thoth added these days to give us our present 365. Thus the link with the Moon and the passing of time is clear. There is also a connection with the Moon and creativity in this story, as the addition of those five days enabled Nut, the Egyptian sky goddess to give birth to her five children, Osiris, Horus, Isis., Set and Nephthys. This answered the problem posed by Ra, the sun god, who having been offended by Nut (and Geb, the Earth deity) declared that she should not give birth during the 360 days of his year. The power of the Moon, through Thoth, comes up with the answer to this. This story also gives us a link between the Moon and the Earth, both concerned here with fertility and birth. We shall make a little more of this connection in due course.

At this juncture we must also pay homage to Isis, regarded as the greatest of Egyptian deities. Isis is also regarded as the perfection of motherhood and feminine power. She was the only one to gain the knowledge of the secret name of Ra, the sun god, obtained by tormenting him with poison from a snake. It is interesting to note that this knowledge would give her power over life and death. In part Isis' connection with the Moon and our interest here, comes from her taking to the constellation of Sirius, the brightest in the sky. In the previous chapter we saw that Sirius is called the dog-star, whose image as the tamed wolf we now know. The view of Isis as the archetypal mother further strengthens her link with the Moon. Also her name has been described as an onomatopoeic derivation of the sound of crying, linking her with the Tarot card of the Moon, often shown with tears, as symbols of emotion and the effect of constant change, like the process of life, with which we must each come to terms. So the Moon then had a central role in the beliefs and lives of the ancient Egyptians, their lands being viewed as a reflection of the heavenly abode of the gods they could see above them.

To the Greeks the Moon was the goddess Selene, sister to Helios, the Sun. The waxing, growing phase of the Moon was likened to the growing of the pregnant woman's womb, and the position of the Sun and Moon at the time of the New Moon to the copulation of man and woman. It is also a common belief that the power of fertility was reflected or held in the horns of the New Moon, many deities coming to be depicted with these horns. Thus the Moon came to be associated with fertility and growth, which has since been confirmed by scientists, as the Moon is now known to affect fertility, fluidity and plant growth. We will look further into this aspect of the Moon,s influence upon us later in the book.

For now we need only recognise the close relationship between the mythological beliefs concerning the Moon, with fertility and the Earth itself. For as is popularly believed, these myths have their basis in fact and through them we can trace the development of the human psyche or soul and thus its relationship to the world around us, of which we are an intrinsic part. That the Moon is associated with fertility is shown through mythology by the many deities that have dominion over agriculture, birth and the Earth itself. Humanity has of course, to ensure its future survival by procreating, seen as a sacred act in ancient times.

The Moon goddess then was also seen as the abiding power over the Earth and indeed, the Earth it, or her, self. We must mention here the Greek Earth goddess Gaia, given new importance in recent times by James Lovelock and his Gaia hypothesis of the Earth as a living being. Through this we can then come to view the goddess of the Earth and Moon together affecting fertility, growth, life and death. If then, there is such a link and identity between them, it is but a short step to realising that we can play a vital part through linking ourselves with this power, since we are creatures living upon the Earth and thus part of her being. As the Moon makes its way through the constellations of our sky over the period of a year, so it produces an ever changing pattern of influence and energy to her counterpart, the Earth, that directly affects its fertility, growth and indeed, death, through the movements of its waters and plant life and so on.

With this realisation must then come the awakening to the fact of our role in all this. Through meditation at times specific to the phases of the Moon, we can bring ourselves into coordination with this energy and power and utilise it to its maximum effect, both within and without ourselves. That is, each individual can benefit from doing this and so can the Earth.

We can of course choose to live outside of this awareness, living in ignorance of such energies, gods and goddesses and things that glow in the night! Once the path has been started upon however, there is ignited in the individual a small but brightly burning flame that is apt never to go out. He or she then begins a lifelong process of initiation into the esoteric or inner world of spirituality and magic, as opposed to the outer world of materiality, comfort and, in many cases, hedonistic excess. This is known to those on the inside as the exoteric and more is said about this process in Chapter 4.

Returning to Moon deities, the Greeks can introduce us to the idea of a triple aspected goddess aligned to the three phases of the Moon, that is waxing, waning and Full. To each of these phases was assigned a deity, according to female fertility - virgin or maiden, bride or mother and crone or hag. These changed according to the phase of the Moon.

The first phase was the New Moon when the goddess was a young maiden, beautiful and virgin. Then She has a child-like aspect and it is good to view and interact with her as a friend at this time. As the Moon grows, so does the Goddess mature and show more of her face to us. By the time of the Full Moon She is the Mother in full bloom, full of common sense and understanding. It is possible to commune with Her as such, but it is necessary also to honour any commitment you make. She only reveals herself to those who open themselves to receive Her inner light. As the Moon wanes, the Goddess ages and becomes the hag or crone at the dark of the Moon when Her face is turned away from us. She is now the old wise woman, dark, sinister but knowledgeable in human and magical ways. There are many detailed and interesting aspects to this, some of which are explored in 'The Magic of the Moon'.

The first waxing phase of the moon, from new moon to the beginning of the five days when it is considered full, was to the Greeks' Artemis. When the moon shone, Artemis watched over them, and animals and plants would dance. At the village of Arcadia young girls would wear a phallus to ensure their fertility. She was often depicted as a naked huntress, virgin and vengeful of any male who looked upon her. She was the protector of small children and assisted at childbirth.

The mother aspect of the Greek moon goddess was Demeter, as queen of the Earth and linking us here with the growth and fertility of the land. Demeter had to embark on a search for her daughter Persephone, who had been abducted by Hades, god of the Underworld. Demeter placed a famine on the land, failing the crops until her daughter was found. It was eventually ruled by Zeus that Persephone should spend one third of the year with Hades, the rest with her mother.

Lastly with the Greeks, the goddess Hecate, 'the distant one' was the magical and enchanting aspect of the Moon, identified as the aged but wise old woman. Hecate defended children and was strongly connected to regenerative and maternal powers. She had a positive influence on farming and agriculture, being typical of many Moon deities in this. She was also queen of the dead and linked with ghosts, another sign of the mystery surrounding the Moon and the attitude of awe towards her. Statues were often found of Hecate at crossroads, where she would appear to travellers with her pack of white hounds. This gives us another link between the Moon and the canine world, dogs here being sacrificed at one time to Hecate. This triple aspected goddess has a similarity to Celtic beliefs, as we shall see.

We have already met Cerridwen, the Celts' corn goddess, as the corn spirit containing the wolf. Here we can establish the connection with the Moon, once again through the growth and fertility aspect of the crop and the land from which it grows. To the Celtic peoples who inhabited many parts of the British Isles, the Moon was also a goddess with three aspects or faces. There were many different tribes amongst the race of Celts, and since they were a migratory people, they had many different conditions under which to live. This gave rise to localised gods, with different names allotted to them. We can however trace unified beliefs, one being the triple aspected goddess of the Moon. The differing aspects of these have been explained above, but we can here introduce ourselves to an interesting psychological view of these deities.

If we view the Triple Goddess as an archetype, that is the original mental image upon which we shape our commonly held beliefs, we can place certain psychological types upon each aspect of the goddess. Thus the Maiden becomes the instinct of the human system, natural and unknowing, beautiful in its simplicity. The Mother becomes the Rational or logical, the considered, planned and calculated part of us that seeks to achieve a definite end. Lastly the Crone becomes the intuition or inspiration, as its has its source in the unconscious mind, the dark and usually hidden depths but that contain the wisdom we need, if we would but allow ourselves to hear it. We will explore this relationship further when we consider the three phases of the Moon, as it has direct relevance to the way in which we can work with the power of the moon, through the Triple Goddess, to achieve our wholeness.

To the Celts the 'science' of numerology was of great importance, the number three being a sacred and powerful number for them. From this we find that if we multiply this number by its own power i.e. three, we get the most potent force of nine. The Celts attributed this power of nine and three to their Triple goddess. They also had the legend of the Cauldron of Rebirth, identified also with the Holy Grail. The contents of this cauldron - water, giving us another link with the power of the Moon which controls all water - was said to have regenerative and healing powers and it is watched over and warmed by the breath of nine maidens, identified as our Triple Goddess in her various guises.

The ancient Celts also had their own alphabet, based on the properties of trees, that thus formed a sort of seasonal calender as well. That there were thirteen consonants in the alphabet is thought to have been the basis for the thirteen months in the Celtic year, which were divided by the passage and phases of the Moon. This was later adjusted to our present calender by the Romans, at the time of the conquest under the Emperor Claudius.

Another interesting aside it is worth mentioning here is that of the Celts beliefs concerning the Unicorn. They considered that this beast was endowed with certain powers, partly through its horn. This was said to be coloured white, red and black. These align themselves to the Triple Goddess just nicely. White is the Virgin, pure and clean; red is the Mother, fertile and bleeding with her monthly - or lunar - cycle and black is the Crone, dark and mysterious. Robert Graves tells us that this power was centred on the dog-days, Sirius, whose relevance we have already seen. An interesting feature of the unicorn was that it could not be captured by any other than a virgin, in whose presence it simply laid down. So as we can come to tame the wolf, perhaps certain of us will meet this fabled creature!

Such was the importance and power of the Moon to the ancient tribes of this land and others the world over that an eclipse of the Moon was seen as a time of great strife and danger. The Goddess was thought to have turned Her face away and thus Her blessing. The Moon was seen as the counterpart to the Sun, on which survival depended, for its warmth and ability to make things grow.

In *'The Golden Bough'*, J.G. Frazer explains how the Roman goddess Diana was the equivalent to the Greek Artemis and was worshipped as the mate of the 'King of the Wood', the personification of the power of the Sun and God of Nature. His power was seen to wane and die each year, being reborn with the return of the Sun in the spring. Diana was the goddess of the woodlands and had her sanctuaries in groves, principally that at Lake Nemi in Italy, just north of Rome. Her power continued throughout the year, being impregnated by the King of the Wood to ensure the fertility of the land and thus the survival of the people. Diana was also identified as the Moon and especially the harvest Moon, giving produce that would in turn give survival through the winter. Thus the King and Queen were married each year, the personification of the Sun and Moon. It is this sacred marriage that is acted out in today's magical rituals and may well have been the subject of the mummers plays that were passed down throughout history, to survive in some form today.

It is interesting to note that many gods and goddesses were really the same figure, with dominion over the same or similar attributes, but in different places. As Diane was also Artemis, both moon goddesses, so was the ancient Greek moon deity Cybele identified with Rhea, their original Earth Mother. Cybele was also Inanna, the moon, love and fertility goddess of the Canaanites. Inanna became Ishtar, the Mesopotamian goddess of love and fertility. This name becomes lengthened to Ashtoreth, the moon goddess of Phoenicia in the Middle east. From Greece again we have Io, a priestess of the goddess of the sky, Hera, who in her turn becomes the Roman Juno, goddess over childbirth and marriage. Io is later identified as Isis, the great goddess herself.

Thus the opening statement that 'all gods are one god' becomes clear - in this case the object to which we return time and again, is the Moon, shown as the source of so much belief, mystery and power. What I hope to give then in this book, is a way to 'tap into' that power, reveal a little of the mystery and in so doing, establish a way of working that can benefit each individual who partakes and by this, aid in the healing of the Earth, which as we have seen, is so closely bound up in the mystery of the Moon. For it is by the efforts of each and every one of those individuals, causing and embracing the change from within that results from such working. The individual becomes a friend facing those hidden depths represented in part by these deities and so is a little more whole than before.

Change must come from within and so as each one changes, so does each contribute to the collective identity, the whole, which then affects the Earth itself. For as we are truly creatures of the Earth, part of the living being of Gaia, so we share in her energy and power. By harnessing this power and directing it to the healing of the Earth, through the energy and power of the Moon, so do we fulfil perhaps the single most important task the human race faces in this period in our history.

History has shown many times that these gods are not dead, but are alive. If not in the forces of Earth and Moon which we have discussed, then in the traces and vestiges left by those beliefs in the collective and individual minds of those who live in this time. Esoteric teaching tells us that we each choose to incarnate at specific times for specific reasons. As we move towards the induction of the Aquarian Age, we must again recognise the importance of our role upon this Earth as guardians of the planet and put right that which our ancestors, the world over, have knowingly or unknowingly, done wrong through pollution and ignorance. It is not right however, to lay the blame fully on the doorstep of those who we see often accused of causing the damage done to the Earth. We must each recognise as more important the opportunity we now have to play our part fully in the successful transmutation of our planet and people into the Aquarian Age.

Further study of both *'The Golden Bough'* and *'The White Goddess'* will reveal the importance of Moon deities and worship and of the intrinsic ties with fertility, the essence of life and survival, through the Earth as a planetary being and the land itself. There are however, other lands that considered the Moon as important and we must make mention of some of these now.

In the Northern, Scandinavian lands because of the different times they appeared, the Sun and Moon were regarded as having the opposite qualities to many of the other beliefs around the World. This does not invalidate them of course, instead allowing us to see other aspects of their characters. In Norse mythological creation tales, the Moon, and the Sun, were the beautiful children of Mundilfari. The Moon leads the way, deciding when he will wax and wane, to tell the time for men. The Sun, as we know is accompanied on its path by two wolves, giving us a link between the Sun and the Moon, which as we shall see in a later chapter, is important. In addition to this, the Norse peoples gave several names to the Moon, all of which give us clues to their view of it. It is known variously as 'Whirling Wheel', 'Rapid Traveller', 'Gleamer' and 'Time Teller'.

To the North American Indians, the Moon was known as Grandmother Moon, immediately telling us something of the importance with which it was viewed. This is partly because of the respect the Indians held their elders in. The advancement of earthly years was regarded as a sign of maturity and wisdom. To the Indians the Moon was viewed as governing all crops, particularly corn, on which life depended. The Moon was also thought responsible for giving dreams and visions.

Some tribes, such as the Pawnee, used the Moon to predict the weather. The Pawnee called the Moon 'Spider Woman'. Many tribes also used the Moon as a calendar, giving appropriate names to each Moon cycle, that would give a guide to what was happening in the natural world, e.g. Budding Trees Moon, Corn Planting Moon, Leaf Fall Moon and so on. These names are given in the meditations for each Moon that follow. These names serve to illustrate for us the intrinsic connection for the Indians between the moon, fertility and the Earth. The moon also gave the Indians power and knowledge through dreams and visions, vital to their decisions in daily life. To the Chippewas, each moon through the year came under the auspices of one of the four Spirit Keepers of the four directions, or the four Elements. This is the equivalent of the Earth, Air, Fire and Water signs in our own zodiac. Thus the moon comes to dictate the very powers of life, such are the Elements.

In the Christian religion, the pagan ancestry of this country and its deep rooted connection with the natural world still manages to hold some sway. Easter is regarded as the time of the death and subsequent resurrection of Christ, possibly the most important time in the Christian calender. The time that Easter occurs is the first Sunday after the Full Moon that occurs after the Vernal or Spring Equinox, which itself falls on March 21st. This in turn, was a time of vital balance in the pagan calendar, when the twin forces of dark and light were equal.

The Old Testament view of the moon was also an important one. Psalm 89 verse 37 refers to it as “the faithful witness in the sky”, while Psalm 8 verses 3 - 5, in explaining how God created the sun and moon above man, says he is “crowned with glory and honour”. Paul in his first letter to the Corinthians says that “the sun has one kind of splendour, the moon another”, showing perhaps an awareness of their masculine and feminine nature. To these early Christians, the previous deities and the closeness to nature must have remained for some time, their lives being that of fishermen and farmers. Thus the passage of the moon in the night sky was of importance, its light being needed, and it seems, still venerated and celebrated. In the letter to the Colossians, Paul tells the converts “do not let anyone judge you by what you eat or drink, or with regard to a religious festival or New Moon celebration”.

Many other religions have aspects that are associated with the Moon. In the East the festival of Wesak is looked upon as the time of the Buddhas birthday. Legend has it that at this time, somewhere in the world, Buddha, Christ and all the masters gather to invoke a great spiritual force, as a culmination of the years cycle. There is also the Islamic Ramadam, a lunar cycle of fasting. We have an interesting view of the ability of the moon to fertilise from the Islamic religion. The area the religion arose in is known by them as the ‘Fertile Crescent’, which is reflected in the emblem of the crescent moon and star that represents this faith. In the Jewish religion, the time of the Passover feast is set as the second full moon after the vernal equinox.

The beliefs concerning the Moon are then deeply ingrained in many cultures and religions the world over, through their myths. If these myths are indeed the story of the human psyche, it is our ancestors who have written the historical aspect of that story. We can now have the opportunity, through working with the Moon and thus linking ourselves up with the editors of the story, the gods and goddesses, to write the next chapter.

We have seen that there are many, many countries around the world whose spiritual and religious beliefs centre around the Moon, being seen as specially related to women and to fertility, thus controlling the very power over life on Earth itself. In certain ancient beliefs, the Moon was thought of as being the agent that impregnates the woman, with the 'horns' of the New Moon. Elsewhere women who wanted to conceive would sleep with their bellies exposed to the light of the Moon. In Africa, the months are set by the moon and are named by the characteristics of the phases of the moon, such as 'bean harvest' and 'first rains', similar to the American Indians, showing their recognition of their dependence on these natural forces.

What is given here is only a brief introduction to the mythological associations with the Moon, which are many and varied and all of which add something to the overall view we have of it and its influence upon us. There are many other cultures with Moon goddesses and gods, as well as aspects of other deities that relate to the Moon. Further study will show that the many more moon gods and goddesses of the world generally have involvement with love, fertility, both of people and the Earth, and the passage of time. Those interested in pursuing this line of study further than there is room for here will find their efforts richly rewarded. We however, must move on in our journey to the Moon.

3. THE MAGIC OF THE MOON

The mere mention of the word magic immediately causes many people to recoil in horror, their minds and imaginations filling with images of chanting witches standing naked deep in the woods, bringing about infernal evil with their spells, potions and rituals, the odd unfortunate animal lying about in sacrifice to their demons.

Nothing could be further from the truth. Any witches standing naked in the woods of these islands must be very hardy folk, for it is apt to be chilly even on the warmest day in Britain. Quite apart from this, there is absolutely never any sacrifice or remotest harm done to any living creature, be it animal, human, plant or whatever. Witches, pagans, magicians, wizards or whatever other label you care to use to describe those who practise magic, revere all life and have due regard and respect for it. It would be easy for me to digress into a defence of all that is good and positive about magic, for indeed, much harm is done by such images as described above, to those who seek to express their spirituality in this way and bring a little of the ancient sacredness back to our modern lives. However, with the exception of the preceding sentence, I will leave such defences to the courts, where in recent times, the absurd allegations of child abuse and such like, have been rightly and properly disproved.

The purpose of this chapter of the book is to show the importance the role of the Moon has upon magic and so on our very life's structure. For we will see that magic is intrinsically bound up in the very way our lives are shaped, in part by the Moon. In doing so, perhaps I will be able to finally lay to rest any dark fears you may have about the practice and purpose of magic and in this way, tame a little of your own wild wolf.

Magic then, has a place even in the most scientific of lives, whether we like it or not. The definition of what magic actually is has caused much consternation amongst authors of magical titles, each having their own particular interpretation. This would seem to suggest that magic is an individual art, each taking from it what he feels he needs. This of course, requires responsibility on the part of the practitioner, as to the methods and goals of their magic, but those seeking to betray the very high laws of respect, non-interference and goodwill, would soon find their efforts falling on 'barren soil'.

One thing that is clear from the various definitions of magic is that is has to do with change. This is change on any level, be it the most mundane, practical change in the daily schedule of one 'insignificant' person, or the most awe inspiring change that effects the lives of a whole country or continent. Magic permeates the deepest recesses of our minds and bodies and brings all things into the light of self examination and truth. Through this, we must learn to live up to the responsibility of maintaining the planet on which we live and taking care of one another. Magic can assist us in this apparently impossible task in many ways, none of them mysterious, sacrificial, or threatening. Magic uses natural principles, or the principles of nature, to achieve its ends, we being part of that nature.

Nature, or as magicians often see it, Mother Earth, is in a state of constant change, through the annual process of birth, growth, decay, rest and renewal. Here we stand in the midst of this change, these days trying to master and control those forces, with dams, defences and satellites. Whilst it is clear that technology can in many cases be seen to be necessary for the preservation of life, too often we are finding that the methods of this technology pollute nature and obstruct her forces of change. It seems to me sensible to concentrate on utilising and harmonising her power and (re)learning to flow with it. It is clear from many recent events (the Mississippi flood, the Sydney fires, the Bangladesh floods, the Texas droughts etc. etc.) that this natural power is an awesome force, capable of great beauty and great destruction. Anyone who has stood at the edge of the Grand Canyon, seen the landscape from Glastonbury Tor or simply watched a sunset over the sea has seen this power for themselves. All the time, it heralds change.

We cannot obstruct change, it will happen and in the way that nature perceives suits her best. This can cause pain and death, as we have seen throughout history, so surely it is now time to respect and live with this force and energy, as our distant ancestors did, with their ancient magics the world over. For magic is, literally, as old as the hills. This does not mean that we all have to abandon our safe houses and convenient technology, but that we must adapt it so that it blends with the controlling forces around us. We must, in short, save ourselves. It is not the planet that is in danger of destruction, but the human race. If we continue to threaten and pollute the planet, then she will have no alternative but to remove us, like a bacteria, from her body in order to save herself. How many of us would give our own mothers poison?

It may seem that this takes us a long way from the Moon and meditation, but we shall see that in fact it takes us to its very surface. If magic is, as Dion Fortune puts it 'the art of causing changes in consciousness' then meditation, surely, is magic. Anyone reading this book who already meditates will know that meditation can, and usually does, result in a change in consciousness. For those that do not yet meditate and wonder what on earth a change in consciousness is, simply practice the exercises given in this book, beginning with the Grounding and Connecting exercise, and you will find out!

The 'consciousness' aspect of our definition is covered in more detail when we examine exactly what meditation is and how it works later in the book. The 'change' aspect is what we are now concerned with. Change then, as we have seen, is the province of nature, or Mother Earth. She can be seen and approached as a Goddess, the governess or mistress of change. How she brings about those changes, and how we can try to assist her in this momentous task, is where Full Moon Meditation comes in.

As we have seen, the Goddess is the goddess of Earth and Moon, intrinsically linked with fertility, life, birth - and so change. We could perhaps view the Moon as the agent of change upon the Earth. It is well known that the Moon affects the waters of the Earth and controls the tides, which in their turn, have a great effect upon the Earth. This will be examined in more detail later, as will the relationship our bodies have to all this, being 'bags of mostly water'. For now, it is sufficient to know that the Moon has a direct effect on this aspect of natural change all around and indeed in us. So if we align ourselves to this change, through the process of meditation at times specific to the Moons influence and position, we can see that we can exert a great influence to help bring about the required effect those changes wish to incur. This then, is the magic of Full Moon Meditation.

These changes then, are in part, brought about by the movement and passage of the Moon through the heavens. The ancient science of Astrology divides the heavens into sections that constitute the Zodiac. Each of these zodiacal signs are said to personify, or give emphasis to, a particular type of influence or energy, that effects each one of us. This is in turn dependent upon what planet is where and also of the position of the planets at the precise moment of our birth. As the moon makes its way through these twelve sections of our sky, so it adds its own individual nature or force to these invisible energy rays that are constantly beaming down to us. This relationship and 'dance of the heavens' will be explored more when we look into the Astrology and Astronomy of the Moon. We can see already however, that by putting to use the energy we find inherent in our own bodies, our 'life-force' if you will, we can combine this with the same energy that exists on a much wider scale from the Moon (as it does from all the other planets) and direct it, through the concentrated use of our will.

This use of the will is indeed magic, for as many of the magical books in my bibliography will tell you, it is precisely through concentration and the directed will that magical thoughts, wishes and spells are able to manifest into plain physical reality. How they do this is conveniently appraised in the principle 'Energy follows thought'. Thus we find that we are able to, quite literally, create our own reality. What we think, is what we are. This happens on many different levels. How many of us have found that if we consider ourselves as worthless, unable to achieve things, so we feel unable to bother even trying, and we give up before we start. Rather, if we tell ourselves that perhaps we could if we really wanted to, climb that mountain, or write that book, we begin to feel that maybe we will achieve something worthwhile, that even if it does not completely fulfil our wildest dreams, at least we can say we tried. Though it follows the same principle, this goes much deeper than positive thinking or the idea of 'where there's a will, there's a way'. This is however, closer to the truth than many of us think, as we shall see.

If we take this principle and the energy that goes with it, up to the level of the working of nature and the influence of the Moon upon those workings, we can see that we are able to take a positive and helpful role in their outworking. For any who may be wondering, it is perfectly possible to work against those forces and tides, but such workings have no place here and I will therefore make no mention of them, save to acknowledge their existence. We are here concerned with working with the forces of nature, and helping to 'heal the wasteland' and also improve our quality of life, bringing us into alignment with natural forces once more. Just as the principle of 'energy follows thought' applies to each individual being, so does it equally apply to each planet and all the planets as a whole, i.e. the Universe of which we are an intrinsic and vital part, just as the heart and lungs, blood and bones etc. of our bodies each have their own individual and unique role to play and together constitute the efficient or otherwise, working of the body.

The recognition of this relationship between the individual and the whole is an important one for us here, as it is another magical principle with which we must familiarise ourselves so as to fully understand what is happening when we meditate with the Full Moon, and when we meditate at any other time.

I have hinted above at what may be termed scientifically, Newton's law that 'for every action there is an equal and opposite reaction'. Substitute 'energy' for '(re)action' and we enter the realms of magic. This energy or life force is the very stuff of life, the invisible but very real 'substance' that esoteric teaching tells us originates in the mind of God. Just how it affects us when we meditate is best left to the chapter on physiology, but for now we will see how it has its place in the magical world of the Moon.

If this energy comes from the mind of God, or the Source or the Divine, or whichever label for convenience you wish to use, then in one sense it is 'God'. For from all these thoughts came creation itself, came the world upon which we live and all that is in it, including ourselves. So if this energy is able to bestow life, as it truly does, then it follows that it must be alive itself.

Just as this energy is alive, has force and potency to effect things - to bring about change - so do we share in that power. This is not some lesser shadow of the same energy that created the world but a vital and valid part of it, just as the various parts of the body are vital to its health, as previously illustrated. It is an intrinsic, equal part of it, that shares the same source, potency and capability. Thus we reach the principle that what is within us, is also without us, or what is above us is also below us.

These two maxims, from American Indian and ancient Western traditions respectively, both have many different meanings and levels of interpretation and we are concerning ourselves with only one part of the whole here. But it is a part that contains many clues as to the real power and effect we can have upon our world and ourselves, without and within, when we meditate with these natural forces.

We may like to term these natural forces the 'complementary opposites' of the effect that the moon has upon us. This energy we are talking about flows down to us in perpetual motion from the depths of space and through into our atmosphere and thence into our bodies. So as we share in this energy flow from the wider Universe, so there is an energy flow within and around our bodies. This system of energy, encapsulated in the aura and the chakras (see Chapter 4), can be viewed as a smaller counterpart of that wider energy. If then this wider 'Universal' energy came from the mind of 'God' it follows that it came about by the concentration and applied thought of 'God'. (Please excuse the inverted commas every time 'God' is mentioned, but I am not yet sure what or who this 'God' is!) All creation then came from these thoughts and manifested out of this energy, and so 'energy follows thought'. Since we each have this self same flow of energy happening within us, it follows that we too exemplify this principle. We too then, are able to create our very own world. Or, in other words, we can create the reality we want and need in this world.

This happens, as has been mentioned, by the concentrated application of thought and its directed vision through the will. It is accepted these days that we do have an energy field around and through our bodies (this again is explored in 'The Moon and Us'). Each organ of the body, including the mind, also has its own energy field, which is like a tiny replica of the 'Universal' energy of creation. When we meditate we open ourselves to receives a greater influx of this Universal energy. This combines with the thoughts we hold in our minds, together with the emotions we feel, to create an energy particle, or 'blob' if you will, that is then sent, by the energy of those thoughts, out into the big wide world, where sooner or later, it is changed into a living reality.

The details of this procedure are explained in the next chapter, but this is the essence of how it all works, of how we are indeed able to create our own reality, just as we want it.

Before you begin to have visions of manifesting a large stack of shining gold coins and a sprawling 30-bedroom mansion, I must remind you that in order to do this, we must be working in accordance with the principles upon which this energy is founded and works. These are the laws of nature, which as I pointed out at the beginning of this chapter, are more powerful than we are. To attempt to work against them, for selfish gain, is like trying to slow a car down by accelerating - you are simply working against the natural way things are created to work and as such are wasting your time. With a little faith and patience however, you will find that the way of service, of which we shall speak more later, has its own rewards. It is easy to say that such rewards are beyond comparison with money, property or big cars etc. but until you experience this for yourself, you will not appreciate their true meaning.

If you are reading this book, the chances are that your heart does not lie in such materiality anyway. If they do, then please give these natural forces and principles a chance to operate in your life and then try and say that the money or possessions you have gained from your workings is worth more than the peace and well-being. If you truly feel this, and it is possible to do so, then you are working against what is natural, and have chosen to turn your back on yourself. Another principle of nature is freewill and in these times we must each make the choice to work for our own gain or for the good of the planet. To paraphrase my favourite 'sci-fi' series, do the needs of the many outweigh the needs of the one?

Just what these natural principles are, the human race seems to be still struggling to discover, but here we may concentrate on one that we know to be true - that of our old friend change. And indeed we must make that friend of change, for with him on our side we are able to adapt to and flow with it in as smooth and harmonious a way as seems possible. Once again, we find that we must face, accept and welcome something that is difficult and wild - we must tame this particular wolf too.

This change, as we know, is brought about in part by the Moon and her movements. It does this by the directed flow of energy to specific places of the Earth and of our own beings - as distinct from mind or body. It includes both these, and indeed the spirit, as we shall see. By opening ourselves quite literally, to this flow of energy, and then directing it with the concentration and directed will of the mind and indeed the body that follows, we are then able to assist in bringing about the necessary changes nature or Mother Earth would wish to make on her own body at specific times.

Just as then we participate in this wider aspect of creation, at Full Moon intervals, so we will find that in our own lives and bodies, we will be participating and taking an active role in creating our individual lives the way that we would want them to be. This does not mean that we become like gods and are able to lord it over other less powerful beings, but merely that we are once again fulfilling the responsibility we were given many thousands of years ago, which has been recognised and then forgotten. Now, with the onset of the move into the Aquarian Age, we have the opportunity to re-learn this and many other lessons to make our lives more fulfilled and the Earth our true Mother once again. This is indeed, magic.

All these references to the way in which meditation is magic and applies the changes Nature wants to make are general at this stage, and in Chapter 6, concerned with Astrology, we will see how we can specify the nature of these changes, confident and sure that they are in accordance with Mother Nature's wishes.

Having made the effort to acknowledge our much maligned mother, it would be a terrible wrong to assume we know her mind. Humility is a great and necessary quality that must accompany us on our journey. For the remainder of our time in the magical realms, we will examine some other ways in which that silver world can be utilised and applied in other ways and means.

We have already examined the way in which the Moon is a goddess to various pantheons of belief across the world. Many of these beliefs associate magical abilities with the power of the Moon. Consequently there are many magical arts that have been associated with the Moon for a very long time.

For many of today's Pagans, witches and magicians, the Moon is a goddess, a female force or deity whose influence is a subtle, inner, soft and flowing one. She controls our emotions and feelings and gives us our dreams. She bestows psychic abilities and inspires us with poetry. Many poets think of Her as the Queen of Poetry and regard Her as the muse, the haunting and beautiful lady that gives them words from out of the mist of illusion. She is also known as the White Goddess and has associations with many animals such as the hare and horse. In these subjects alone there is a great deal of information and indeed, power. I would refer interested readers to Robert Graves' '*The White Goddess*' for a full and magnificent investigation into this aspect of the Goddess.

The use of the Moon, and her power as it comes to us through its different phases, as well as its general influence is an ancient and potent one in practical magic. Included later is a suggestion for a practical magical working of your own. Magic, though it has its roots in the very creation of the human system and being, is a subject that is able to adapt to the changing times and vagaries of human traits and times. Indeed, its very essence is this change, as we have seen.

Though the methods and tools we use today are based on ancient principles, they are being adapted to blend with the view of the world we are unfolding for ourselves as we move to the next millennium. Perhaps in this we may find some clues as to the way in which technology may be married with nature. Long ago, however, daily life was more immediate in its connection with Mother Earth and survival often depended on it. Consequently, those who understood and worked with this power were viewed with awe and not a little fear.

The old Wise-Woman or Cunning Man, the village witch common in our older communities, would pay attention to the phase of the Moon when collecting herbs for their healing spells, medicines and such like, knowing what the best time for planting, harvesting and so on was. Gardening by the lunar phase is still used today, though sadly not as an accepted and 'normal' practice. The links that this practice give us with the Moon and nature are however, important in our investigation here. The Moon moves through a different sign of the Zodiac every two or three days, thus emanating a different influence to the Earth and all upon her, according to the properties and characteristics of that sign. These signs receive their power from the Sun, the moon reflecting its light and therefore its energy and power. Plants, vegetables and herbs therefore can be deliberately imbued with an exact power and energy, specific to the use the gardener wishes to make of them.

The time of harvest is all important as to the properties captured and concentrated in the plant. Those plants harvested under the light of a Full Moon are apt to have their power and energy increased, whilst those gathered under a waxing Moon are best used in magic for drawing energies in and attracting items to oneself, whether these be practical, emotional, mental, spiritual etc. Therefore, those plants harvested during a waning Moon are best suited in use for distributing energies and ridding oneself of unwanted illness, thoughts, feelings, associations etc.

The logic here is quite simple. As the Moon waxes or gets bigger, so it pulls toward it and sends to us an increasing energy and as it diminishes or wanes, so it lessens in its influence over us. These powers and energies are radiated down to the Earth, and all that grows in or on her, in accordance with the 'phase' or power of the Moon. These are ancient principles then and very basically given here, but do serve here to illustrate the way in which the Moon's phase and influence can be utilised in such basic commodities as the fruit and vegetables and the natural medicines we use. As an example of the way in which magic can adapt to new thought and the progress of the human race, as I write this chapter I read of a magazine article that details the way in which the Moon's light is being captured for use as a Homeopathic remedy.

In order to experience this light in its proper context and to feel it fully within, it is necessary to escape the neon glow of our towns and streets. Under the light of the Moon and in the quiet of the country lane or in the open field we can be still and gaze upon the face of the goddess above us. There it is possible to commune with Her and pay Her due regard. In our scientific world we have lost touch with the power of the Moon and the help She can give to us. This is not to say of course that the power and influence is not still at work and affecting us in our daily lives, nor is it impossible to re-establish that link and become aware of it once more. By meditating with the different phases of the Moon, as well as the Full Moon itself, we are taking a big step in that direction and opening ourselves in some degree to the Moon's flow and energy in our lives.

We can of course increase this connection immeasurably if we are able to leave the comfort of the armchair and the 'security' of our towns, cities and villages. If we are open to letting ourselves be led, with a simple request in our minds to the Goddess, she will indeed lead us to her, guiding us to those silent places that do still exist, even in the midst of the busiest street. Many of the ancient sites of our native lands are now surrounded by roads and electric lights. Whilst this undoubtedly takes its toll, it is still possible to experience the magic held there, cherished by the god and goddess. The first such ancient site I encountered and grew up living close to is now a Victorian fountain, encircled by a three lane road. Yet still, at night under a clear sky with the moon hanging bright over the sea close by, there is still a silence amidst the roar of the traffic and the sounds of many people.

It may seem strange to speak of silence amidst the roar of traffic, but I am able to tell you that it does exist, regardless of the level of physical noise around. I am able to tell you this by experience and for you to understand how and why this can be so, you must have your own experience. To truly encounter the Goddess in this way, it is indeed necessary to wander in the dark lanes and through the woods of your local environment. Here, you can come face to face with the goddess, whether of Moon or Earth. For us, we will concentrate on the Lady of the Moon, who is apt to change her appearance and thus be 'all things to all men'. She does this through the phases of the Moon and by filling us with wonder, awe and respect.

In the New Moon phase, when there is the crescent looking as sharp as can be in the sky, speak to the Goddess as the Maiden. This is the child becoming a woman. She can become your friend, who can help you and even play with you. Now she is virgin, innocent and full of that wisdom children have without knowing. She is honest like the child, sometimes painfully so, but always seeks to help, never to hinder. Her energy reaches out, just as the child's hands reach out to everything within its grasp, to explore and to make contact, Respond to the outstretched arms of the Goddess at this time and she will accept you with love and with trust. Be true to her and you will gain a friend for life.

As She grows feel Her energy grow within you, awakening your insight and awareness. It will rise like the tides and you will begin to recognise yourself moving in tune with her rhythms. Together you will feel the changes sweeping through the land, from within. In time you will see that those inner changes are mirrored in the changes you see around you in the natural world. When She is Full, the Goddess becomes motherly towards you, and rises later in the night. She brings inner understanding and common sense. She may treat you like a stranger unless She knows you as one of her children. For, like any mother, she feels the needs of those she knows as her own, from deep within her being. These, quite instinctively she will protect and supply. Their needs come before her own, and with the Full Moon hanging swollen and heavy in the sky, her giving energy and unconditional love is shared for all who would make the journey to receive.

In the waning phase we look inward and seek out the things that come from within. Now we serve Her purpose as best we can, acknowledging our femininity, whether physically male or female. In the dark of the Moon, the Lady is wise but sinister and unforgiving. Now we can banish what we would be rid of, whether external or internal. The Goddess is now the wizened old woman, apt to be more selfish and aware of her due respect and wisdom. We must be careful to treat her so. Now is not a good time for performing magic as the force of the Crone can carry you away, unless you are aware of her subtle workings. From here however, she turns full circle, literally, and becomes the beautiful maiden once more, smiling down at us from on high.

These phases and their magical influences have a direct parallel with the Triple Goddess beliefs of the ancient Celts who inhabited these lands and many others in their nomadic existence. In this we can find a way that the ancient beliefs of our ancestors still have relevance today and that the gods and goddesses of old are still alive, their hearts beating steadily under the tarmac, between the neon and amidst the squalor and deprivation so needlessly wide spread these days. In this alone, hope can be reborn in many a heart.

In magic, such arts as divination and scrying come under the auspices of the Goddess and the power of the Moon. The word 'scry' comes from 'to descry' which itself means to 'catch sight of' or to 'discover by looking carefully'. It is most closely associated with gazing into a crystal ball, but this is in fact a more modern version of using a dark mirror to see symbols, scenes and portents, arising from out of the mist. By focussing in a relaxed way on the surface of the mirror or crystal ball and concentrating on a question or subject in the mind, it is possible to 'see' symbols, scenes or pictures pertaining to what you have asked. The technique, like many such things, is a knack that requires much patience and practice but it is a natural ability that we are all born with and not the province of initiated witches. By calling on and sincerely and humbly asking the goddess to assist you, using whatever name for Her feels right for you - perhaps 'Lady of the Moon', 'Queen of Midnight' or simply 'Moon Goddess' - you will find that She does respond, if you pay Her due thanks afterwards, regardless of what you experience. The scenes are always there, you have simply to become aware of them.

It is also possible to ask the Goddess to give you dreams, for She rules over this strange aspect of our night-life too. By concentrating again on a subject about which you need to know more, before you go to sleep ask Her to show you a dream that will answer your need. Think of this as you gently drift off to sleep and you will find, that if you wake gently, your dream will be revealed. Always take a few moments to give your thanks, regardless of whether you have become aware of anything or not, for you may not discover the content of your dream immediately. It may be buried within the mind, under the influence of the Goddess of the Moon.

It is perhaps worth mentioning here that we do dream every night, not only on those nights when we remember our dreams. The way in which we wake is of great significance as to whether we are able to recall our dreams or not. Those that are wakened by the ring of the alarm bell or the blast of the digital clock will find great difficulty in bringing their dreams to conscious awareness. Those who are able to allow themselves to wake naturally will find this process much easier.

As you lie gradually becoming aware that you are awake, though not quite, it may still feel as if you are in your dream world, wherever that might be. Indeed you are, and it takes only a very gentle and soft effort of will, as you become aware of the outline of the room you are in, to bring your dream up to the level of your everyday, waking consciousness. It is a good idea to jot down the essence of your dream, for even as you lie there relaxed and warm, though you may think your dream is safely caught in your head, it may well slip away, forever to be lost in the lands between the worlds.

Those that think they may never wake, or wake too late to get to the office on time, if they do not set their trusty alarm clock are mistaken. It is a simple process to tell yourself what time you wish to wake, as you go to sleep and you will discover that your natural body clock will respond to this. Close to the appointed time, you will wake. We are creatures of habit and after some nights of telling yourself what time you wish to wake, you will be able to go straight to sleep, confident in the knowledge that your body clock will ring your own internal alarm when it is required. I wonder who controls this clock?!

Another magical practice associated with the Moon is the ancient and powerful ritual of 'Drawing Down the Moon'. This involves three women, or possibly one man and two ladies, reminiscent of the Triple Goddess once again. The ceremony is performed outdoors during the first three nights of the New Moon, or the Full Moon. This usually takes place just after sunset as this is the only time that the New Moon is visible to us. By catching the image of the crescent of the Moon in a bowl of natural water, it is possible to use this for a communion or to scry in and so form a deep link with the Goddess of the Moon. This ritual shows us a direct way of working with the energy and power of the Moon.

We have already seen how magic as 'the art of causing changes in consciousness' has an immediate parallel with the Moon and its influence upon us. The Moon is forever changing, appearing at different places in the sky night after night and showing us a different face each time. Through this seemingly random and compelling dance, the moon comes to be associated with the Trickster, a figure from traditional symbolism who is the border between the conscious mind and the sub-conscious. Here the light plays tricks and deceives us, just as moonlight can do.

This brings us to the use of divination in magic, with the Tarot. The word divination really means to make a contact with the Divine. The Divine is many things to many people, whether the Christian God, with long white hair and beard or simply a being without form but incredible power. The Divine may have many different aspects, personified by the gods and goddesses of old, and it is to one such aspect that we concern ourselves here when we conduct our divination, that of the goddess of the Moon. Here She bestows psychic ability, insight and intuition, speaking to us in symbols and prompting us from our sub-conscious mind and heart.

In the Tarot, perhaps the most widespread (and misunderstood) of the divinatory arts, the Trickster is also the Magician. He attempts to make changes to his immediate environment and he can also deceive and beguile, according to his whim. He too stands at the border of the conscious and sub-conscious mind, for he has just been the Fool, as in the 'Seekers Quest' of the Tarot, the journey of each spirit or person, is depicted in consecutive cards through the Major Arcana. The Fool is the beginning of all things, the dim memories we have of our origins and that which is our basic make-up. The Fool can represent the sub-conscious in psychology, making the Magician, the first and immediate experience of the Fool, on the border between the conscious and sub-conscious. In this way is he controlled by the Moon, seeking as he is to be a vessel through which he can direct a higher force and manipulate this to control his life.

We will also meet and see the significance of the next card in the sequence of the Major Arcana of the Tarot, card number 2, the High Priestess, later in our journey. The Moon is also able to influence changes within us, not only in our consciousness but physically, as we shall see as we wander and explore the surface and body of the Moon, looking at ourselves in the process.

4. THE MOON AND US

In this chapter we will continue our metaphoric journey to the moon, this time as we draw closer, examining its surrounding energies and examining our own bodies also, looking at the relationship the one has on the other. Through this we will see just how intrinsically bound up we as humans are with the natural world and with the movement of the Moon, its different phases and therefore, its energies. We will also see how we can adapt our lives to that of the will of the Divine.

To fully see the effects of this, we must begin thinking regularly that 'thought is energy'. Those skilled in the esoteric or occult arts, or proficient in meditation may well be aware of this procedure already. For those who are not, you will find that to begin considering all things as having their equivalent in an energy form is the best means to establish this awareness. As creatures of habit, we humans are quite adaptable and easily convinced. You will find it will take only a short time of conscious thought to establish this idea, which we explored in the previous Chapter, as a standard means of examining and considering your actions and thoughts.

As an example to illustrate the process of this idea, let us suppose you wish to send healing mentally to someone. You may well be worried about this person, but the phrase 'worrying about it won't help' springs to mind, here with an accuracy all too meaningful. If what we think becomes reality due to the energy of those thoughts, then it follows that the negative thoughts we have, and they can be many, are as powerful in force and effect, as those positive and helpful things we think, say and do. If therefore we wish to heal someone, we do not think of them with their illness or dis-ease in mind, for if that is the image we concentrate on, that is the reality we are sending them. If however, we picture them as they ideally should be, in full health, or perhaps receiving healing energy, in our minds eye, then that is the physical reality we are giving them. It is necessary to create a positive 'thought-form' in order to help heal someone in this way.

The phrase 'thought-form' gives all the meaning we need to explain our principle here, as we have already seen that thoughts do indeed, become form, just as the technical plan and drawing of the architect becomes a physical reality in the hands of the builder and carpenter. If all things have their energy equivalent then, so too, does the Moon, and we will now explore the way in which the energy of the moon affects us physiologically, in normal circumstances, and when we meditate.

It is a well known and accepted scientific fact that the Moon acts like a magnet on water, thus creating the tides of the seas and oceans. Those that live close to the sea or tidal rivers will perhaps be more aware of this than others, but we can all feel the ebb and flow in our bones, if we make ourselves aware of these subtle yet powerful influences. This is because our blood has the same chemical composition as the water of the oceans - in other words, they have the same things inside them.

Growing up as I did beside the sea and being a frequent visitor to watch the sunset and the moon rise, a most magical operation, I can testify to this with confidence. If words on a page are not enough for you however, and there is no reason they should be, then you will need to make some effort to feel these tides fully. Spend time sitting beside the water, whether of coastal origin or inland river.

If you become calm, and with patience and regularity, you will begin to sense and to feel these rising tides within you, rising literally like waves of emotion and passion within, giving you feelings you did not know you had, and causing responses within that may make you smile and weep, perhaps together. If you are prepared to sit beside the watery veins of Mother Earth you will seek out, and find, your instinctive connection with nature and will come to realise the part you play in all of creation. This has to be experienced, it cannot be planted as an idea in your head, much like meditation.

All living things contain water in varying degrees, including humans. Our bodies are approximately 65% water and so we feel the pull of the Moon to a large degree. We have water in our blood, in our saliva, tears, and to ease the movement of joints. We feel this pull, like gravity in our bodies, from the cells that make up our bodies. Other species too feel this energy and instinctive reaction and it is worthwhile to observe pets at different phases of the Moon to see what effect it appears to be having on them. It is also good to observe our own feelings, behaviour, dreams and instincts in relation to the Moon's phases in order to see just how much we are affected by the Moon. You could keep a Moon Diary, in which you place thoughts, feelings etc. you have observed, alongside a note of the phase of the moon. This need only take a moment and can be kept with you at all times in a small notebook, for future reference. You may surprise yourself at what you discover.

Mental patients are known to be more disturbed at the time of the Full Moon and it is commonly known that the origin of the term 'lunacy' to describe those unfortunate enough to be deemed 'mad' in the eyes of society, has its origins in this observed effect. This comes form the Latin 'luna', from where we also get the slang 'looney'. It is thought by some that if those who controlled the regulation of the institutions of this country could learn to work with the effect of the Moon, embracing the views of the esotericist, the therapy used within could be enhanced and the path back to sanity made smoother and more understanding given to those apparently on the wrong side of normality.

We can see in this association of the Moon with madness another aspect of the fear of the unknown we seem to cling to. The Moon has since ancient times been believed to have the power to inflict great influence upon humanity, either for good or bad. When good, it has the power to stimulate growth and even bestow life, through its associations with fertility. When bad however, it can bring madness upon the individual and ultimately destroy life. It can bring the onset of seizures, induce trances and drive people to suicide. The instances of those believing themselves to be transformed into werewolves are fact, not fantasy or horror. This interesting effect of the moon upon we humans is a separate study by itself and so we will not divert out attentions in this way. Instead I will refer interested readers to Nigel Ashcroft-Jackson's work *'Call of the Horned Piper'* for an introduction to this.

One of the many superstitious beliefs concerning the Moon was that to sleep exposed to the light of the full moon would drive you insane and that to have the moon light shining on your face would leave you 'moonstruck'. This is a state of becoming entranced or trapped by the Moon's influence. Although harmless, it renders the victim an ineffectual and apparently idiotic life for its duration.

Many early physicians and doctors, such as Paracelsus, believed in the powerful effect of the Moon on their patients, noting especially its maximum effect when new or full. This correlation with a particular phase of the Moon even crept into the law of the land, with the *Lunacy Act of 1842*. This allowed for the lunatic to be sane during the two weeks prior to a full moon, but deemed insane for the other two weeks. Reasons for this madness have been widely postulated, with suggestions including the gravitational pull of the moon effecting an adverse reaction in some people. This takes us back to the effect the Moon has upon the human body. Not only does it effect the fluids of the human body, but it has a scientifically proven effect upon birth. More babies are known to be born when the Moon is Full. Science has also shown that there is also a lunar cycle to the variation of the acid and alkaline levels of our blood.

Statistics also show that there are more suicides at the time of the Full Moon. These unfortunate people are thought not be in their right minds at the time, because of the Moon's effect upon them. It is believed by some today that the Full Moon causes a particular response in the electrical activity of the brain, which has been linked with epilepsy. There is much evidence to link the moon power with epilepsy, going back as far as mythological times with the Greek goddess Selene threatening epileptic fits to those who annoy her, from medical literature through the Middle Ages and beyond.

Much work has also been carried out recently on the relationship between the phase of the Moon and its effect on a woman's menstrual cycle. The duration of the complete Moon cycle falls roughly into the same time bracket as a woman's menstrual cycle. This is a very specific and important study, beyond the scope of this book and my knowledge. I would therefore refer readers to the book '*The Lunar Cycle*' by Francesca Naish for a complete study and guide. We can however, make mention of the way in which women can align themselves in this way with the power and energy of the Moon and so capitalise on the effect in meditation.

Many people believe these days that the cause of much misery and alienation felt in our big towns and cities is due to a lack of contact with nature. Certainly, the rampant spread of our grey, concreted world has drastically altered most people's lives and the subtle, soft influence of birdsong and the sound of insects singing at night has become a whisper against the roar of traffic. Women can however, find a deep and primal contact with nature once more, through aligning the cycles of their bodies, through the menstrual cycle with the phase of the Moon. This takes a little effort, as explained in '*The Lunar Cycle*', but once established, will allow those women a feeling of the sacredness of this time, rather than it being a painful, unwanted infliction. An instinctive connection with the Goddess can also be achieved in this way.

Those women who choose to do this may also find that it will increase for them their experience of Full Moon meditation. Where however does that leave men? Men are now portrayed in the advertising world as subject to the guile and planning of women, needful of rippling muscles and a square jaw to be a 'man'. The roles have become reversed once more and the balance we really need slips from our grasp again. Some research has however, been done into men having a lunar cycle. This focuses on the sperm count, results suggesting that this is markedly higher at specific times during a man's lunar phase. This phase is particular to each individual, dependent on the angle of the sun and moon and the movement of the two. This is explored in the next Chapter. If then, the Moon can have an appreciable effect on men's ability to be fertile, the very basis of life and creation, it is not so daft to assume that men are affected emotionally by the Moon as well. This thought I will leave for each person to ponder, but it may provoke some interesting marital discussions!

It is alleged that by finding out the precise phase of the Moon at the time of her birth and avoiding making love at that time each month a woman can utilise the Moon as a natural contraceptive. The details of this practice must be observed and adhered to, as detailed once more in the valuable book 'The Lunar Cycle'. We can see from this of course that we can choose the time we wish our babies to be born, as well as plan when to conceive. Thus the nature of our child can be partially chosen, using the principles of Astrology. Basically, if the Moon is in a 'positive' astrological sign during conception, the signs of Aries, Gemini, Leo, Libra, Sagittarius and Aquarius then it is more likely the child will be a boy and if in the other signs is more likely to be a girl. If the Moon is close to the border of two signs then it could be either boy or girl.

This study of the link between the Moon ability to affect fertility and birth has many fascinating aspects, not least the result that once the individual has attuned themselves to the movement of Natures phases, they have, in effect, aligned themselves with the planet itself. If we return to the belief of 'Gaia' or Mother Earth as the living, breathing personification of the planet, then as we

2
THE HIGH PRIESTESS

become intrinsically linked to the fertile and infertile phases that surround us, so we become chemically and biologically part of the planet, and thus the goddess of the Earth. This, as we have seen, applies as much to men as it does to women and it is a thought worth much meditation alone that we are each indeed part of the body and total being of the goddess that is our planet. This being the case, it seems to me that given the number of people in the world today, each one therefore being a vital and equal part of the goddess, how powerful and magnificent She is. As the one who is able to give life through this fertility and therefore truly our Mother, we must ask ourselves why we see fit to ruin and pollute Her the way we do. As I have asked before, which one of us would daily give our own Mother poison? Equally, How much instead can be achieved through giving our Mother love and healing. We are able to see these things in so many ways if we but tried. One such way is the practice of full moon meditation.

This relationship of the moon's effect on both female and male behaviour and biological function, can be seen to parallel a basic esoteric principle of which we should take note at this stage. To do this we must introduce ourselves to the next figure the Fool becomes in his journey through the 22 cards of the Major Arcana of the Tarot. We have seen how he first becomes the Magician, as the outer, active masculine principle, seeking power and control. This mastered he goes on to meet and become, the High Priestess. Here we have the inner aspect, the personification of intuition and the feminine nature. Here the Fool learns understanding and his inner ways.

The Priestess sits, guarding the entrance to the lands beyond the veil, the unconscious mind and the land of dreams. This is equated to the feminine power and mystery, with which the Fool must familiarise himself. In actuality the Fool is neither 'he' nor 'she' but hermaphrodite, or of both sexes. He begins his journey containing the physical nature of both sexes and containing also the energy and power of both natures. By dividing them, the Fool learns the secrets of each, through the Magician and High Priestess. Interestingly, his next persona is the Empress, known as the embodiment of Mother Earth. Thus the Fool has learnt the secret of creation and life and is able to align 'his' life accordingly.

The High Priestess is then the personification of the unconscious part of the mind. The Moon makes an appearance on this card, to show its link and influence on the unconscious. The High Priestess is shown with a crescent Moon on her brow, showing this directly. She also has a crescent moon under her foot. This is not to demonstrate that she suppresses its force, but rather is in touch with it and allows the energy to flow through her.

The duality of male and female is a subject that has much relevance to our practice here. Esoteric teaching tells us that this duality or 'complementary opposite' force is contained in all things. Just as there is male and female there is night and day, black and white, birth and death. More meaningful to us, there is also wild and tame, Sun and Moon and New and Full.

Each of these principles is the equal and opposite of each other and we must each seek this balance within ourselves if we are to find peace and well being. In every female there is an inner male and vice versa. This is a mystery that can become familiar, just as the wolf can be tamed to become the dog. Just as through reading this book you will come to learn the ways and means of working with the Full Moon in meditation. You can be said to be initiating yourself as a Priest(ess) of the Moon. In this way, the unknown, hidden or exoteric physical planet in the night sky becomes a force, energy or power within and without you, as an esoteric law by which you live, having an identity as a goddess.

These dual aspects are reflected in so many ways in our lives and have often been portrayed in films as a battle between good and evil, the archetypal forces of light and dark. I would venture to suggest however, that it is not a battle but a balance that is being striven for. Just as nature moves from more light in Summer to more dark in Winter. so at specific times there is balance between the two. The wheel then turns and the delicate interplay between these male and female principles is acted out.

Upon the outworking of this balance all life depends and so we can see why we must all find this balance within if we are to play our full part in maintaining it. As we shall see, it is the interplay of the Sun and Moon, as the personification of the male and female forces, that we are dealing with when we align ourselves, in energy form, during our meditations. Through the combination of their energies, as they affect us at specific times through the year, we can assist in maintaining this balance on the planet and in the Universe and giving ourselves in the process the means to achieve alignment with this inner peace and well being.

Once you have adjusted your awareness to take into account the phase of the Moon, you will find that many things fit the pattern of its changing force and influence, from general energy to ability to concentrate and fertility. It should be remembered that these things are subtle, like all such things at this level. The Moon's pull on you will not enable you to run twenty miles one day where you could run only one the previous day, just as you cannot actually see the tide increasing. It will affect your mood and feeling, just as at high tide the water seems more alive and vibrant - able to travel further - making us tidal beings in our own way.

In the body, the Moon specifically is said to influence the function of the digestive and lymphatic system (the system that controls the movement of fluid around our bodies in white blood cells) and synovial fluid that lubricates the mechanism surrounding our joints. The Moon also affects the breasts, ovaries and pancreas. The pancreas is a large gland behind the stomach, which secretes insulin, the protein hormone that controls the level of glucose in the blood. Glucose is needed to provide the basic energy and warmth that enables us to survive. Those people then who seem to be adversely affected by the Moon may also be suffering from an adverse level of insulin, such as diabetics, the treatment of which could be helped by meditation and visualisation to control the stimulation and flow of this fluid. A low level of 'blood sugar' or glucose is also known to produce emotional instability, giving us come clue as to the validity of 'lunacy' in its true sense. It can be seen then that as the phase of the moon changes so does our basic level of energy, our motivation, activity and 'life - force'.

The overall production of the chemical processes occurring in our living organisms is known as the metabolism. Thus a deficiency or over-production of one or more of these chemicals produces a metabolism that is unbalanced. We have already seen how important it is that equilibrium is maintained in ourselves, as well as in the wider Universe, if we are to maintain physical and emotional well being. The function of the metabolism results in the process of growth, production of energy and elimination of waste. The direct and vital influence of the Moon on this process has been made clear, showing just how important it is to regulate this influence in our lives, through such methods as Full Moon Meditation. It can also now be seen that the process of growth, energy and waste can be equated to the process of birth, life and decay of the human. This is in turn equated to the three faces the Celts and others ascribed to the goddess of the Moon, giving substance to the belief that all mythology has its basis in fact. Thus the Moon controls our whole flow of life.

It is known that some imbalances of insulin levels and the like are hereditary. As the Moon is linked inextricably to physical fertility by its influence on the ovaries and breasts, so it comes to be associated with heredity and our family, especially the mother. This leads us on to the identification Dr. Carl Jung makes with the Moon, which is dealt with in the Chapter on Psychology.

So we can see that the Moon controls the influence of many fluid secretions in the body and release of hormones that effect behaviour and temperament. As we have mentioned, all physical things have their energy equivalent and this physical activity is no exception. It is accepted nowadays that the human body is surrounded by an energy field, auric field or aura. This aura is known to have seven layers or bodies, that each interpenetrate the other, each subsequent layer stretching out further than the last.

The layer closest to the physical body, in both physical dimension as well as density, is called the Etheric Body. This term comes from the word Ether, which is that which exists between matter and energy, which is an apt description of the Etheric Body. Its existence can easily be felt by those with a little sensitivity, simply by rubbing the hands vigorously for a few seconds and then moving the palms towards each other, without touching. A sensation will be felt akin to squeezing a light sponge, as if there is some force that is between the palms, keeping them apart. This is the Etheric Body.

The product of all the physiological activity in the body provoked by the moon, is that the Etheric body, as the energy counterpart of the physical body, increases its level of vibration. Each layer or body of the aura vibrates or moves quicker, in accordance with the wavelength it relates to. Each of these auric bodies consists of millions of tiny energy particles all vibrating or oscillating, like the 'snow' that can be seen on a television screen. Those energy particles that are further away from the physical body move quicker than those closer. The fluids and hormones of the body are energy particles slowed down to the extent that they take on physical form. They are not however, as dense as the bones of the body, which have slowed still further.

If then we turn our minds all the way back to all creation emanating from the mind of 'God', and remind ourselves that 'thought is energy' we can see that we really are no more and no less than this energy ourselves. As such we truly are 'created in 'his' image and likeness', as an embodiment of the energy of the mind of 'God'.

It is then a simple step to realising that in our minds we have the very same energy, in essence, as that of 'God' or the Divine. If this energy is the stuff from which all life came and the planet itself, then how easy it must really be, once we have become used to and accepted this knowledge, to create the world and reality that we truly want.

This increase in vibration of the Etheric body has the effect of making us physically more speedy and energetic at the time of the Full Moon, but also more nervous and anxious. With meditation we can learn to change these negative aspects to positive and turn that positive side into an active force or energy. As the etheric layer of our body vibrates faster at the time of the Full Moon, so more information is allowed to pass through from the unconscious and subconscious layers of the mind to the brain. This is because as those particles move faster, so there are more gaps between them, thus allowing more light, which is energy, to come through to the physical body. This is then turned into the fluids and hormones that affect our feelings and behaviour, and the way we think. Thus at the time of the Full Moon we experience an increase in our subconscious and intuitive thought, the Moon's energy being known to influence this part of our brain and mind, just like the High Priestess in the Tarot.

The Moon is also known to affect many things in Nature besides the human body. Trees felled at the time of the waxing or growing Moon have a greater amount of sap. Maple trees have a charge or energy that fluctuates in accordance with the Moon. Worms are known to turn to the left or right dependent on the phase of the Moon. Rainfall has also been charted in many parts of the world as following a lunar cycle and hurricanes occur mostly at the time of the New and Full Moon.

The breeding cycles of many animals are dictated by the Moon, such as worms, shrimps, some types of seaweed and even coral. Experiments with oysters have shown that they follow a lunar cycle with their opening and shutting. The metabolic activity, and therefore the levels of goodness, contained in vegetables has also been shown to increase and expand during the waxing Moon and decrease during the waning Moon. We can see from this how important it is not to interfere with Nature's cycles and how we can easily benefit ourselves by growing and picking our crops in accordance with the phase of the Moon.

Having seen how the Moon affects the physical changes in our bodies, let us now examine the way in which meditation affects the body and we will then be able to see just how powerful an affect we are able to have, both on ourselves and others, by combining these two and meditating at specific times of the Moon. It is known that meditation causes definite improvements in our ability to handle stress and make us more calm. We become more aware of our own condition and more sensitive to outside stimulus, either positive or negative. These outside stimuli have a pronounced effect on our behaviour as well as physical condition. This is largely controlled by a process in the body called the metabolism. As previously mentioned, the metabolism is the sum total of the chemical processes of the body, particularly the production of energy and the elimination of waste. Meditation can affect us at this metabolic level and so we can regulate and use the energies occurring within us, as influenced by the Moon, to produce optimum effect, for ourselves or others.

Every living thing has energy and indeed, is energy, as we have seen. This of course includes every human being and the Earth itself. It is this energy field of the Earth that has caused so much damage by pollution and this goes on to produce such phenomena as acid rain and the greenhouse effect. So by damaging and polluting the ozone layer we damage the air quality we breathe and so the energy available to us on a daily basis. By damaging and polluting the Earth then, we are damaging and polluting ourselves and 'God'.

We know then that 'thought is energy' and that this energy is the stuff from which our reality is formed. Thus reality occurs first on an energy level and second on a physical level. The principle of 'thought is energy' works like this: We focus our thoughts by concentration and imagine or visualise certain circumstances and influences happening, such as healing somebody of a headache, or sending healing energy generally to a place that has just suffered an earthquake etc. These thoughts, as energy, invisible but measurable and real, then travel, like radio waves through the air and the Earth. As other people concentrate on similar thoughts or for example, visualise healing energy being sent to the same place, so these 'energy thoughts' join together, being of a similar nature to create one bigger thought form or 'blob' of energy. Because this energy 'blob' has a bigger area and more particles being added to it, so its level of movement is slowed. Eventually it becomes so much slower and denser in movement and mass that it becomes too heavy to remain as energy. It begins to crystallise and so takes shape as a physical, tangible reality. Thus, we create our own reality.

The best way for us to create thought forms that are pure in nature and in line with the mind of 'God' and the force of nature, is to raise our consciousness to a higher level, which gives us an awareness of what the mind of 'God' might be and from where we can instinctively know what is correct to do. As our society has become increasingly logical and more automated, so we need to live less and less on our wits and instincts. These however, are our greatest guide and friend. It is at the level of instinct and intuition that our true wishes are known. If we are leading a life of service to the highest source and Divine, trying to fulfil our inherent role of looking after the planet, then we will find that those instincts and intuitions that come to us, when we raise our consciousness through a process such as meditation, will be in alignment with those natural laws and higher wishes.

The same is true with meditation. When, in meditation we change or raise our level of consciousness, by keeping our minds concentrated on directing the influence or energy available to us from the Moon's phase, we can cause changes to occur on an energy, Universal or Cosmic level. This subsequently appears as a physical reality, given our continued application to the matter and correct attitude. This is one of knowing, as opposed to believing, that what we do in our meditations has an effect. Another important aspect to this is the principle of service, of which more shall be said later.

If we then consider the Earth or Universal energy field to be affected at its level of vibration by such factors as the phase and energy of the Moon, we can see how by meditating at one particular phase of the Moon we are able to bring the level of vibration into being as a reality on Earth. We can focus on particular energies, in keeping with each particular Full Moon and by meditating and concentrating, we are able to send these qualities out, as energy, into the world.

In our meditations then we concentrate on the qualities of light, love and healing, which are energies themselves. We then radiate them out to those people, places and situations that are in need. This forms the basis of Full Moon meditation. Light takes the form of colour, which is a visible appearance of energy, moving at different speeds, as explained above, that give it the physical appearance of different shades, as we perceive them.

So by meditation we connect with the natural energies that are around us at that time. We will explore what these are for each Moon through the year, later in the book. For now we need only know that what we send as our thoughts blends with the flow of natural energy that is around us at all times.

This energy, that originates in the mind of 'God' flows in a constant and never-ending stream from the depths of space, from the Sun, the sky, the planets, the stars and of course, the Moon. It is in our air, in our minds and bodies. The energy we radiate at our Full Moon meditations then becomes reality, as explained previously. As energy however, it is not of practical use to us in any tangible sense.

This Earth or Universal energy is therefore translated to a form which is workable within the human energy system, the Aura, by what are known as the chakras. These are energy centres or vortices located at various points around the body, each aligned to different parts and functions of the body and its systems.

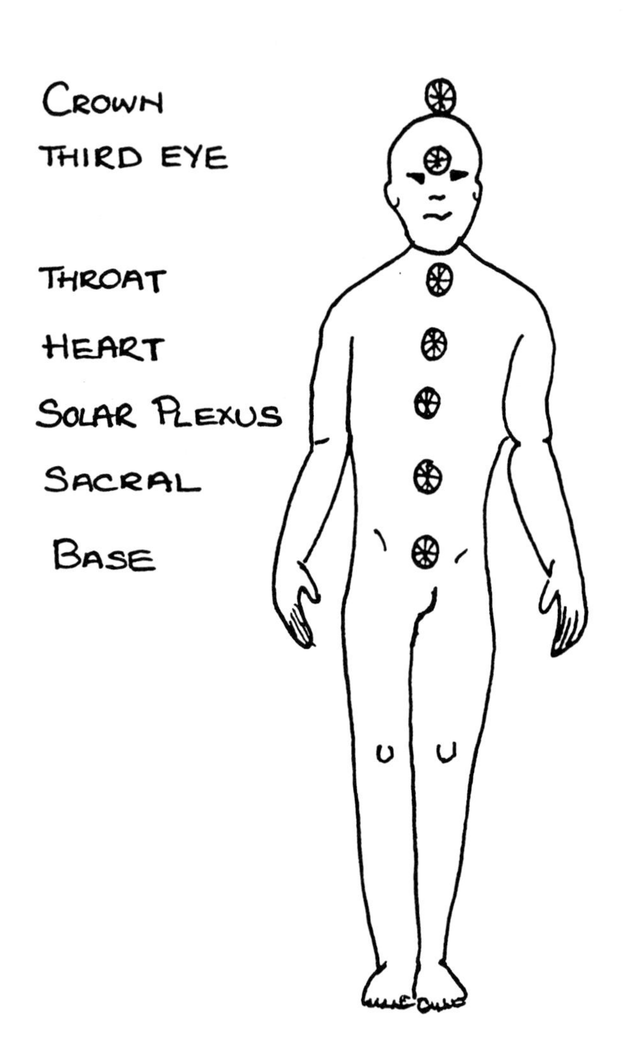
CROWN
THIRD EYE
THROAT
HEART
SOLAR PLEXUS
SACRAL
BASE

There are seven main chakras on and around the body, chakra being a word meaning 'wheel'.

The chakras are thus wheels of energy. When we meditate we are able to open these chakras, which happens automatically to a degree, as we relax deeply. This enables us to receive and distribute greater amounts of Universal energy. There are specific ways to open the chakras, either through meditation or exercise, which are given in many books, dealing with meditation and healing.

The chakra known as the Sacral, situated at the level of the body just below the navel, is the one that controls the fluid balance of the body and so should be focussed upon as the way to absorb and release the energy around it. As the energy passes through the chakras, it is passed to the various glands of the body, such as the pituitary, pineal, thyroid and so on. Each of the chakras is aligned to a gland. Each gland also has a specific function in the body, but we need only know here that they produce and release hormones. These hormones contain fluids that dictate our responses to situations and circumstances and thus greatly affect our behaviour.

The pituitary gland is known to respond to light, including the light of the Moon, which comes from the Sun, as daylight. When it is stimulated in this way, it produces increased levels of 'follicle stimulating hormone' (linking the Moon again with growth). This gland is aligned to the chakra known as the Brow or 'Third Eye'. This is located above and between the eyes, on the forehead and through the body at this level. It is thought by some that in our distant ancestry we did indeed have a third eye, the pituitary gland being the remnant of this, still responding to light as it does.

In some Eastern systems of meditation, the lotus flower, the Eastern version of our water-lily, is seen as a symbol of the Moon, being its reflection and counterpart on Earth. There is an obvious connection with water here too. Opening the chakras is likened to opening the petals of the lotus. The petals of this original Flower of Light (Fleur-de-lis) are also identified with the phases of the Moon. The lotus is likened to the Crown chakra, located on the crown of the head and through which we receive and distribute the highest aspects of Universal energy, higher thought, inspiration and so on.

This relationship also works if we consider and indeed see this energy as light, specifically the light of the Moon. I have pointed out elsewhere how we are all cyclic beings, responding biologically and therefore mentally to the levels of sunlight available to us. It is this light, as energy, that we absorb through the aura, chakras, glands and hormones of the body that regulate our behaviour and responses. As we know, the Moon reflects the light of the Sun. Therefore, when the Moon is Full we see more sunlight than is usually available, during the night. This light is absorbed via the optic nerve in the eye, and acts as a nutrient for the body. These 'extra' levels of energy available to us during the time of the Full Moon, aside from stimulating our dreams, can also be used and directed in the meditative state to people and places in need through the process indicated above.

We can see therefore that by using meditation to invoke, attract, and then distribute the particular energy of the Full Moon we are able to bring ourselves into alignment with that energy. We do not have to be controlled by the phase of the Moon, an unwilling and helpless victim of what the Moon chooses to dish out to us, metaphorically cornered by the wild wolf ready to devour and consume us. Instead we can become vessels by which the Moon can be used to direct its forces and energies to those in need. This, as we have seen, profoundly affects their physical reality. It also affects our own reality, causing us to become aligned with what is happening, unseen, in the world around us and brought ever closer to knowing the true will of the Divine and closer to the goddess that is our Mother Earth.

5. THE PLANET

In this chapter we finally arrive on the surface of the Moon, after our long and occasionally hazardous journey. Now we are free to wander the surface of this new world, exploring, discovering and admiring the view of the Universe we have from here: the stars, the Sun and our own blue-green planet Earth.

The Moon itself has no atmosphere and its surface is covered with craters, mountains and lava-plains, known as seas, although there has never been water in them. These glory in such names as the 'Sea of Tranquillity' and 'Sea of Fertility', which may give us a clue as to the feeling of being on the surface of the moon, as well as the connections with these qualities we now know well. These names were coined by Riccioli, an astronomer of the 17th Century. Good binoculars will give a view of the craters and mountains and it is possible to see the main lava-plains with the naked eye, on a very clear night.

Mankind has been observing the moon for hundreds of years, the first map of it being produced in the early 17th Century, by William Gilbert as physician to Queen Elizabeth I.

It would seem that this monarch had more than a passing interest in matters Universal and occult, also having Dr. Dee, the famous astrologer and occultist as her advisor. In those times, the moon was still seen as a strange and mysterious place, seeming to have an effect on the tides and appearing in different parts of the sky night after night, yet always showing the same part of its surface to the Earth. We will see just how this happens in this Chapter.

The invention of the telescope in the 17th Century enabled some of the mysteries of the moon to be revealed. It was thought previously that the moon consisted of land and sea areas, pertaining to the lighter and darker areas that could be seen with the naked eye. However the telescope revealed that these were in fact mountains and craters, with large areas of plains as well. Some of these mountains reach up to five miles in height.

Observations of the moon and details of its surface gradually revealed more and more until in the 1960's humanity at last set foot on the Moon and was able to see directly what it was like, as well as bring pieces of it back to Earth to be examined. Since those heady times, we have sent many a flight into the furthest depths of our Solar System, with some amazing revelations. Whilst this represents great advancement of knowledge, one wonders as to the effect of the many, many satellites in orbit in the skies now, some with devastating capabilities in event of war, as well as the polluting effects upon the Earths atmosphere and that of other planets. There seems always a price to pay for such knowledge.

The moon itself is virtually airless and is devoid of water. Though it has no light of its own, there have been colour formations observed on its surface. This consists of peaks, sometimes in ranges, sometimes isolated, valleys, plains and marshes. There are also many craters, some very small, some huge. The largest measures 184 miles in diameter. Some craters have peaks in their centre. It is thought that these craters were formed by the impact of meteors, or by volcanic eruption, in ancient times, since there is no trace of such activity now. The craters or seas, were formed from lava flows that became basalt on solidifying. Other names for these seas are: 'Bay of Heats', 'Sea of Crisis', 'Bay of Rainbows', 'Lake of Death', 'Ocean of Storms'. 'Sea of Serenity' and 'Lake of Dreamers'. With the esoteric knowledge we now have we are able to understand these terms on a different level than may have originally been thought.

One feature, with interesting implications for our studies here, is the emanation of bright white rays from the surface of the Moon that come from certain of these craters. These are best seen at full moon and appear like giant spokes on a wheel. Hundreds of these rays flood out, measuring up to 1,900 miles in diameter. There is an area between the craters and the rays, so they do not penetrate the surface. This would seem to suggest that they are flowing outwards. Although astronauts have visited the rays, little is known about them, it being assumed they are thin deposits on the surface. A probe did find an unusually large amount of aluminium at these rays and less iron.

Remembering that all physical things have their energy equivalent, such rays emanating out from the surface of such a planet as the moon, with its undoubtedly massive effect on our own systems and waters, would suggest to my mind that these rays may be the very energy with which we have become so involved. Perhaps we are seeing a physical representation of that which pulls the tides, causes blood to flow, emotions to change and our meditations to be so powerful. Thin layers of the matter of these rays would seem to suggest a fast moving vibration to the energy particles they consist of, making them part energy, part matter - perhaps.

The dominant chemical element on the Moon is oxygen, as it is on Earth, being 42 percent of the Moons atomic structure. There is also aluminium, calcium, magnesium and nitrogen. The Moon, again like the Earth, has a core and a crust, the crust being thicker than the Earth's. The 'soil' on the Moon's surface is about 2 or 3 feet deep and has no organic life. It has been formed by the surface rock being eroded over billions of years and meteorites bombarding it. As they were formed without water, moon rock looks different from that of the Earth. Analysis of this rock has shown it to have magnetism, or in other words, energy.

The light of the Moon does not in fact, exist at all. The light we see is the light from the Sun reflected onto the Moon. This is the reason why, in our meditations, we work with the Sun as well as the Moon. We will examine later the individual nature to each

21
THE WORLD

moon. These are determined by the sign of the Zodiac in which the Sun is positioned at the time of the Full Moon. Thus the influences and character of that zodiacal sign are said to be those influencing us, as they are reflected from the Moon. We are therefore working with both the Sun and the Moon. As we know, the Sun and the Moon represent the masculine and feminine forces and polarities respectively (although vice-versa in some traditions) and so we find that as we work with both of these energies we are able to establish a balance of these forces within us.

If we return to the Tarot and remind ourselves that the Magician and High Priestess are the embodiment of the masculine and feminine, having 'split' from the hermaphrodite Fool, we can see that through their combination we are able to blend them again. This brings us to the last card in the Major Arcana of the Tarot, the World. Here we see the figure of the Fool once more, hermaphrodite, shown in many cards with female breasts and genitalia covered. The Fool has successfully blended these qualities within himself and thus rises above need for identifying them. This needs to be our aim internally, identifying the male or female within, and helped by the process of meditation in this way, combining and harmonising them. Thus the Moon is taken as representing that which gives form to the individual spirit that comes from, and is represented by, the Sun. Therefore the Moon relates to the character or personality of the individual and the Sun relates to the spiritual self or identity.

We will find that this balance is something of a pleasant side effect of Full Moon Meditation as it is through their very essence that we attract a balance of energies to us. Since we work with the masculine identity of the Sun, through the feminine power of the Moon, so we attract a balanced force of equilibrium to our systems and energies.

To return to the Moon however, we know that we see the same part of it all the time, as She revolves around the Earth in a counter- clockwise direction. This comes and goes each month, through the waxing and waning process, but still we see the same surface, in different places in our night sky. This is because the Moon rotates, as it travels round the Earth, which is itself spinning of course. The speed at which each spins results in the same area of the moon being visible from the Earth.

This gives us the infamous dark side of the Moon, for years an unknown area of the planet that held many secrets and fears. When photographs of this part of the Moon were finally taken, in 1959, it was seen that it differed little from the near side we had already examined. However, the fear of the unknown returns to haunt us here, giving us further association with the realm of the wolf. This dark or far side of the Moon is, to us from Earth, in perpetual darkness, as we never see it. Thus it becomes associated with the unknown, fear and the wolf.

The Moon actually takes just over 27 days to orbit the Earth, but the interval between one New Moon and the next is 29.53 days because of the movement of the Earth and Moon themselves moving around the Sun. To be exact the mean or average time the Moon takes to physically complete a cycle is 27 days 7 hours 43 minutes and 11.5 seconds and as seen from the Earth the mean time is 29 days 12 hours 44 minutes and 2.7 seconds. This makes a true or lunar month. The origin of the word 'month' does actually mean 'moon'. The orbit of the Moon is in the shape of an ellipse, or flattened circle. It moves at a speed of 2,287 miles per hour, speeding up to 2,429 m.p.h. when it is closest to the Earth in its orbit.

The Moon measures a diameter of 2,160 miles, making it 27 percent the size of the Earth. It is the interplay of the position of the Earth and the Moon that give us its different phases. We see the New Moon as a slim crescent, barely visible. As the Moon waxes or grows, we see more and more if its surface, until at Full Moon, we see the largest expanse possible from Earth. Then it appears as a complete circle. From then it becomes smaller or wanes, until it goes, literally full circle and becomes the New Moon once more.

When the Moon is directly between the Earth and the Sun it is almost invisible to us. As it then begins to move away from the Sun, we see the crescent shape of the New Moon, which is on the right side of the planet as we face it. It then moves further away, thus revealing more of itself. When it is half lit the Moon is said to be in its first quarter. This is because it is one quarter of the way round on its journey round the Earth. It continues and finally becomes completely illuminated, being on the opposite side of the Earth, thus allowing the Sun to shine directly to it, and being 'full' to us. From here it decreases as it completes its journey round the Earth. showing us less and less of itself once more. This slowly wanes to become a crescent on the left side of the Moon, until it passes the point from where it began, giving us the New Moon again.

These three faces of the Moon, as seen from the earth, give us the three phases, of waxing, full and waning. To this we can add a fourth phase, which we call 'dark'. There is a period of three to four days when the Moon is not visible at all. This was a source of great worry to our ancestors, who thought that the goddess of the Moon had deserted and left them. So they performed rituals and rites to entice her back, thankfully winning her over. During this time, it is often thought wrong or at least difficult to perform magic, as the absence of the Moon is said to bring great confusion in its energies and allow the greatest of illusions through. We will examine these phases in greater detail in a later Chapter.

There are three cycles of the Moon with which we can identify, each having their own particular effect upon us. The first of these is the movement of the Moon around the Earth which is detailed above and is the lunar month as we know it from New Moon to New Moon. The second cycle concerns the distance of the Moon from the Earth and its appearance in the sky at different places, seemingly at random. When the Moon appears to be larger it is closer to the Earth and therefore its power is felt much more. This is reckoned to be as much as 25% stronger at its peak, which tells us that at the time of the Full Moon we can increase the effect of the Moon automatically by 25% or one quarter. The last cycle is the variation of the height of the Moon in the sky. This is because the Moon's orbit is not in relation to that of the equator of the Earth. The Moon thus seems to pop up at different places with a different size, almost nightly. When the Moon is higher in the sky we will feel and notice its effect less than when it is closer to us, as its gravitational pull exerts less influence the farther away it is.

The Moon is the Earth's satellite but its pull on the Moon is secondary to that of the Sun as this is the centre of gravity for both the Earth and Moon. This effectively makes the Earth and Moon a double planet, making the influence of the Moon an equal pull between the Sun and the Earth. Symbolically this relates to the realm of the spirit, the Sun and the realm of the body, the Earth, the Moon perhaps being the means by which we can guide ourselves between them. This is related to the Moon's phase growing from New to Full when it gives birth to the Sun. Thus the unconscious, the Moon, is made conscious, the Sun, within us. When we are able to combine the two, such as when we meditate at appropriate times, we are able to form a link or bridge between them. It is this that gives us true wisdom and enables to fulfil the maxim 'Know Thyself'. So we bring information through from our subconscious mind, from the darkness, into the light of our conscious, everyday mind.

The influence of the Moon upon water is well known and what actually happens is that as the Moon pulls away from the Earth, the force of gravity upon it creates a pull on the water. A second bulge of water is also created on the opposite side of the Earth from the Moon's position, caused by the movement of the planet and the gravity of both the Earth and Sun. With these two movements and the movement of the Earth itself, the combination gives us our tides. When the Sun, Moon and Earth are in line they are therefore pulling in the same direction. This causes the highest tides as there is a greater concentration of force exerted upon the planets surface. These are the spring tides, their opposite low or neap tides occurring when the Sun and Moon are at right angles.

Another is this series of celestial dances we can make mention of is the phenomena of eclipses. There are two kinds of eclipses - solar and lunar. Solar eclipses occur when the New Moon is directly between the Sun and the Earth, thereby cutting off the suns rays. The Moon passes in front of the Sun, and appears to be almost the same size. This is because it is so much nearer the Earth than the Sun. This is a quite spectacular sight, lasting only a few minutes, but with people travelling the globe to see it. It is more common for there to be a partial solar eclipse, when the Moon passes over only a portion of the Sun, though this can still be dramatic.

A lunar eclipse occurs when the Full Moon passes through a point in its orbit of the Earth that cuts itself off from the light or rays of the sun. It becomes swallowed by darkness, which is actually the shadow of the Earth. This shadow is caused by the Sun being behind the Earth, as it in turn faces the Moon, to whatever degree. The colour of the Moon may then become a copper or red, until as long as up to ninety minutes have passed, when it will emerge again. Because there are only two points in the Moon's orbital path around the Earth, a lunar eclipse can happen no more than four times per year. Eclipses occur in a pattern every 18 years, 10 days and 7 hours.

In older times eclipses were looked upon with great alarm and distress. Many ideas as to what was happening evolved, such as the belief that the Moon was eaten by dogs, dragons or vampires and wolves, of course.

All this technical and mind boggling information may not have a direct relation to our purpose of meditating with the Full Moon, but it does help to be able to consciously understand what we are dealing with and just how and why the phases happen as the dance in the heavens become clear to us. This enables us to enter deeper in to our meditations when the time comes, with full awareness and control, enabling us to exert a greater influence and energy.

The time of the Full Moon is thus when the Sun and Moon are opposite each other and their equal and opposite qualities or energies are in alignment - that is, they balance each other perfectly. Thus the male and female sides of ourselves that they represent are balanced as well. This alignment happens in a different way each day, when the Sun sets and the Moon rises. This is the time of twilight, regarded as being the magical hour every day because of the particular underlying energy caused by the Sun and the Moon. Thus, as we have seen, when we are meditating with the Full Moon, we are joining and aligning ourselves with the light of the Sun, according to what sign of the zodiac the Sun is in.

We must then, now turn our attention to our view from the Moon to the Sun and the movements we can observe it makes through the stars, from our lofty position. In closing however, to give you some idea of how far we have already travelled, the Moon is some 238,857 miles from Earth!

6. ASTROLOGY AND THE MOON

As we look out from the Moon, we can see the path of the Sun and the myriad stars in our Solar System. That path and its relationship to the stars that surround it, is the subject of this Chapter, when we will explore the subject of Astrology and see its relevance to meditating with the Full Moon.

Astrology is often regarded as the oldest science. Although the interpretation of the birth-chart, the map of the planets at the time of a person's birth, may involve such 'non-scientific' methods as intuition and even clairvoyance, the calculation of it is an exact, astronomical science. This science has been in existence for thousands of years and has been accepted by such respected figures as Sir Isaac Newton and Dr. Carl Jung. Like many such things, its origins are unknown, but it is thought that it may first have been used by the Chaldeans and Sumerians and spread from there to the Babylonians, Assyrians and Egyptians. When we look back through history, we see that the sciences of Astrology and Astronomy were inextricably joined until the 17th Century. This gives us a good indication that it is not the realm of freaks and idealists, but a reliable and accurate method from which we can learn much, both about ourselves and the wider Universe in which we live.

The principles of Astrology state that each of the planets in our Solar System has its own energy or sphere of influence that affects us. Each planet affects certain parts of our personality and character according to its position in the Universe when we were born. This continues throughout our lives, the 'dance' of the planets as they continually move in our Solar System sending down their influence to us constantly. Imagine if you will beams of different coloured light shining down to each of us from above, affecting each individual a little differently according to that individual's position and place. As such the principles of Astrology follow the theory that there is a higher purpose to life, both here on Earth and in the wider Universe about us. By identifying the underlying energy behind each of the planets we can assimilate this into our characters and use it to enhance our individual and collective development.

If we can imagine those coloured beams of light as part of the energy that, as we saw in the last chapter, is constantly being drawn into our being, through the aura and the chakras, then we can realise just how the planets can play so important a part in the make up of our character, both at birth and at any point in our lives. The individual colour of each planet is seen to have its own particular hue to each individual, between them giving that person what they most need to learn, develop and progress in life.

At this stage it is perhaps important to mention that 'progress' comes in many different forms. If the influence of a planet such as say, Saturn, often seen as a limiting, preventative force, is instead seen as giving us teaching (the planet is often called 'The Teacher') we can begin to see how each planet is beneficial, not full of malevolence and spite. It is vital that our hearts and minds are kept open to learn and to receive such circumstances as the planets guide us to creating, viewing all in life as positive.

The extreme alternative is to become bitter, which can create a wall of hardness in the heart, which only the builder of the wall can break down. This is a painful process that will give the same learning, but in a far more difficult way. How much better then to try to accept what comes our way, not with a forced and false smile that covers a rage and hate, but by looking within, through reflection and meditation, to discover for ourselves the nature of what we have in our lives. There is always good within the bad (and vice-versa!) if we but stop to look.

We have already seen how by meeting at the time of the Full Moon we can utilises the conditions most propitious to develop within. This comes from the intake of energy available to us at this special time. We have also seen how the Moon has a strong physical effect on us as it controls the flow of water, and symbolically this emotional aspect of our characters. By using the principles of astrology we have outlined above, we can bring that inner energy out or up, to the conscious level of the mind. This enables us to further the healing work we are able to do with the Full Moon.

In order to do this we need to understand what the astrological energy of the Moon is and how it affects us, so that we are able to consciously use and direct it. This is called by Jeff Mayo, author of *'The Planets and Human Behaviour'* and fellow of the Royal Meteorological Society, as the 'life-principle'. He surmises the life-principle of the Moon as the 'principle of rhythms through instinctive response, assimilation and reflection'. We know that the Moon moves in rhythms through its course of Full Moon to New Moon and back to Full Moon. We have also seen how we too move in those same rhythms, due to the flow of the water in our bodies, as controlled by the Moon.

If then we have an 'instinctive response' to the Moon, when through meditation we open to receive even greater amounts of this energy, it is but a simple step to realising that we can direct it, through our selves to those people, places and situations that would benefit from a greater dosage at that time. This is done by the process of visualisation and concentration, upon the chosen recipients of the energy.

Remembering that all things have their subtle or energy equivalent, the energy of our focussed concentration creates a conductor that carries the intended influence, in this case a particular Full Moon energy, to its destination. This forms part of our work of service to the Earth and the Universe, the principles of which will be looked at in a later chapter.

This then sets out the first two parts of the method of our Full Moon meditation. We need to open ourselves to receiving the flow of energy from the Moon, retaining and holding it, rather like building up a concentration of force. The energy of the force is then released and directed to who or where ever the group concentrates on. The third and final section of the meditation is the time for personal reflection. This process will be explained in detail prior to giving you the actual meditations.

In order to fully utilise the influence of the Full Moon in this way it is best to have a conscious understanding of the nature of the Moon. We have already explored this in some detail and the simple fact that you are reading this book means that when you have finished you will have gained that awareness (I hope!). In this chapter we can add to that knowledge by looking at the interpretation and understanding of the Moon, as seen through the eyes of Astrologers.

The planets then each have a basic function that affects our lives. It is this function that is the astrological interpretation of the Moon. Before we look at the Moon we must remember that the Moon obtain its light from the Sun and so we should look first at the astrological view of this fiery globe.

The Sun is taken as giving us our basic life-force or energy. Its principle is surmised by Jeff Mayo as 'self-integration', giving us the ability to complete our being. The Sun is seen as the governing force of the astrological system we have, being at the centre of the system and therefore symbolically, ourselves.

As each of the planets is aligned to differing parts of the body (an application we can be aware of in our meditations through the year) we can understand from the above why the Sun is linked to the heart, as the central force of the human body. It is also associated with the circulatory system, as linked to the heart circulating blood and energy around the body. Finally in the body, the Sun has a connection with the thymus gland in the endocrine system, in turn then linked to the heart chakra, bringing us back to energy. This vital energy is that which determines the general state of health or otherwise in the body. The thymus gland is also thought to relate to the process of growth and the onset of puberty.

Each of the planets in astrology is defined by a symbol, that for the Sun being a dot within a circle. This represents, amongst other things, the Sun at the centre of our system and the individual within the Universe, which the Sun governs. Psychologically, the Sun is taken to represent the collective unconscious (see next chapter) and the processes by which each individual integrates into the rest of humanity.

Another of the astrological influences the Sun has upon us is through the sign of Leo. Each of the planets is associated with one or more of the twelve signs that the Sun moves through on its passage through the stars. The twelve signs that make up the Zodiac each have their own associations with basic attitudes, ingredients and characteristics in the human. In other words, the planets are the source of a particular energy and the signs are the channels by which that energy is translated into human expression.

Some of the most significant attributes of Leos that we will attract to ourselves through these meditations are self-expression, energy and assertiveness. The symbol for Leo is the lion, full of fire and activity. These powerful traits can become too intense and over bearing, but here we are working with the energy of the Sun through the Moon, so this danger is not one to concern us overtly, as it is cooled and tempered by the feminine nature of the latter.

The Sun is also linked to the fifth 'house' of the birth chart. The practice of placing twelve equal divisions or 'houses' over the map of the birth chart is done to enable us to identify where within us the 'life-activities', effects and impulses of the planets and signs are directed to. In other words the houses show us what we have an urge to do in our lives. The fifth house relates to the need to express the self creatively, in whatever way, and the pursuit of happiness and pleasure, good things indeed to attract to oneself.

We may take a moment out here to explain that the Sun is burning hydrogen, which keeps it alive. This hydrogen is classified as Element No. 1 in chemistry and is the basic matter out of which all other matter is formed. When that basic matter is burned, it then turns into the energy, as the Sun's heat and light, with which we are dealing in our meditations. Without this we could not live. Thus the Sun truly is the source and centre of all our lives.

If then in our meditations we are receiving significant amounts of the above influences from the Sun we are able to see how we can benefit ourselves through participating regularly in them. We naturally attract growth, integration with others, self-understanding and a strengthening of the heart and circulatory systems of our bodies, from the inside out. Also we gain in our awareness of what makes us tick, what we enjoy and what gives us pleasure. This applies to each and every living thing on our planet, that can be helped by us in this way.

We have seen that the Sun plays an important part in Full Moon meditation, as it is really the position of the Sun that dictates the particular individual nature of the Moon's influence we receive each time it is full, owing to the position of the Sun reflecting certain of its light to us via the Moon. We can then think of the Suns energy and influence as being refracted through the Moon.

The Moon complements the Sun's influence by animating its force into action. It gives expression to the impulse of the Sun. The Sun is thus the masculine, active, outgoing force and the Moon is the necessary balancing 'complementary opposite' force of the feminine, passive and introspective. Thus the movement of the Sun and Moon can be seen as the union of male and female, each needing the other to exist and develop, just as the male sperm needs the female ovum. By meditating with the Moon we are not giving ourselves an imbalance of the feminine, as we know that the influence of each Full Moon through the year depends upon which sign of the Zodiac the Sun is in. Thus we have the balance of the masculine and feminine. This is also reflected in psychological terms in the Anima and Animus. For an explanation of this see 'Psychology and the Moon'.

Astrologically the Moon is associated with our rhythms and ability to flow effectively. Therefore the Moon is viewed as the mediator of the flow of time, how we are able to adjust from past to present to future. The Moon directly affects how we are able to assimilate each new experience and feeling into our lives and react accordingly. If we are unable to adjust, then we become prey to the influence of the Moon, rather than regulating and flowing with it. It is then that we become lost in the illusion of the Tarot card 'The Moon' we have already examined: we fall under the Moon's spell. It is then that the wolf turns on us. The Moon affects us at this instinctive level and any blockage here can result in a tendency to cling onto and even live in the past. We need to maintain a flow of experience and appropriate emotional response. One way in which we can ensure this happens is by aligning ourselves to the phase of the Moon, both at New and Full phase. Thus our bodies and minds are realigned and revitalised. This then takes the place of restlessness and irritability.

The Moon is also linked to the sign of Cancer. The symbol for the sign of Cancer, is the crab, linked with water, which as we know has much to do with the Moon. Those born when the Sun is in Cancer have a tendency to be emotional and intuitive, two qualities which are identified as being affected by the Moon. The Crab is said also to resemble the human breasts, which we have seen are linked to the Moon. Cancerians are often easily hurt and very sensitive, though they may not give this impression. Meditating with the Moon will then develop our sensitivity. Cancerians have an instinctive need for security and they have a deep need to regulate their emotions. Through our Full Moon meditations we will help ourselves establish where our security comes from and enable ourselves to better cope with or 'handle' our emotions.

The Moon is also linked to the fourth house. The fourth house relates to the need to make one's home and base secure and stable. It is thus a place of security and protection and is thus connected to the family and parental influence, once more linked to the Moon's influence. The fourth house also 'rules' roots and foundations, showing us that the placing of the Moon is important in establishing the very basis of our psychological make-up.

The symbol for the Moon is, perhaps predictably, the crescent, which in part is obvious in its use. In traditional symbolism the crescent shape also suggests the evolving individual spirit, a principle which blends intimately with our purpose here. Once evolved the crescent becomes the complete circle, the Universe, the Sun and infinity.

In the physical body the Moon is linked to the movement of fluids and the lymphatic system. Therefore it plays a central role in nurturing, nourishing and protecting the body, like a Mother, as these are the functions of the various fluids of the body. The Moon is also linked to the pancreas, which regulates the sugar level of the blood, the effect of which we have previously examined, but which if imbalanced results in emotional turbulence and unpredictability. By moving with the tides of the Moon we can instead regulate these emotions, as we know.

Obviously we have gained a much greater knowledge of the Moon and its influence through these pages so what is mentioned in this chapter is only part of the way it affects our lives. From even this briefest of mentions however, we can see that through our Full Moon meditations we bring to ourselves greater understanding of our emotions and needs, greater security and foundation together with increased intuitive and instinctive powers.

These are basic introductions only to the influence of Astrology upon our beings and lives, which cuts to the very roots of every person's life. Those readers wishing to explore this subject in greater depth are referred to those astrological books listed in my Bibliography and recommended to consult a qualified astrological counsellor.

We have already mentioned that the Moon has no light of its own, instead reflecting that of the Sun. As we know, this is why we are able to see the Moon in its different phases, according to the angle it makes in relation to the Sun. The phase of the Moon is therefore ultimately determined by the Sun. It therefore follows that each time the Moon reaches its peak, the Sun has moved to a different place in the sky. Thus each time the Moon is New or Full, the time of our meditation, it is emitting a different influence to us, depending on the sign of the Zodiac it is in. Thus, when the Sun is in the sign of that name, at the time the Moon is full, it is known as the Libran, Sagittarian and so on. The principle influences therefore of each Moon are in accordance to that of the Zodiacal sign the Sun is in. These influences are given with the suggested Meditations for each Moon.

We know then that twelve differing basic types of energy are being 'beamed' down to the Earth, in succession through the year, dependent on the position of the Sun and the Moon. These energies are related to the properties assigned by the science of astrology to each of the twelve signs of the Zodiac.

In our meditations then, we can focus upon the qualities and influences of the relevant Zodiacal sign and concentrate on bringing those down to the Earth and distributing their positive qualities or energies through the force of our meditation, by concentration. It is important to understand at this stage the reality of the 'thought is energy' principle, as it this that gives us the understanding necessary to make what we are doing most effective.

We can also become aware of and use these qualities to align ourselves with the changing energy of Nature through the year. This makes us more attuned to the natural world around us, able to adapt to the needs of the changing seasons and able to live in harmony with the Earth and with ourselves. Many of these attributes are a natural 'side-effect' of meditating with the Moon, which can be looked at if you wish, as reward for the self sacrifice that plays a part in such a system.

Thus far we have travelled through space and landed on the surface of the Moon. We have explored the planet we have landed on and looked further out across our Universe. Now it is time to dig down beneath the surface under our feet and turn our attention inwards.

7. PSYCHOLOGY AND THE MOON

We must now take our exploration of the Moon beneath the surface and look at the psychological aspects of what we are doing when we meditate with the Full Moon. This is important in helping us to be fully aware of the effect the meditation has upon our being, so that we feel we can trust the process and understand it to the highest possible degree.

Much of modern psychology and in particular that which relates to spiritual subjects, draws on the work of Dr. Carl Jung. Originally a pupil of Freud, Jung went on to effectively create his own branch of psychology and one that included and paid due heed to the occult and spiritual worlds. Many writers have subsequently drawn on his work, which provided invaluable fuel for gaining widespread acceptance for practices such as ours.

Jung produced a great deal of study on subjects such as dreams and in particular the role of symbols, as applied to the different levels of the mind. He explained how the human race can work on a collective as well as individual level. At this 'family' level we are dealing with our sub-conscious minds. The sub-conscious mind retains all the information it encounters, positive and negative, from birth to death. It chooses which to pass on to the conscious mind and into the brain and which to keep to itself and keep hidden. Therefore if we are able to access the sub-conscious mind of a group of people we can influence them at the collective level.

It is for this reason that the energy, or life-force, created by one individual in meditation can be seen as achieving a total greater than the sum of its parts in a group meditation, such as we perform at the Full Moon. By bringing our sub-conscious minds together to open at the same level, through meditation, we are able to tap into a deep source of energy within and without ourselves. This is then directed and joined to the energy emanating from the Moon itself and we have a vital part of Full Moon meditation.

Jung also taught that the sub-conscious mind has its own language, which is that of symbols. Symbols need no language or other information to accompany them to be understood by humans the world over. We respond to them instinctively or sub-consciously. In the modern world of advertising we see that corporate images are used in the same way. Multi national companies now rely on an image more than the company name for consumers to identify their products. This is a very powerful use of symbolism, which it would benefit those unwary consumers to make themselves aware of the effects of. The next time you walk down your local shopping centre, just observe the number of symbols used, rather than words and you will appreciate the degree of their use.

Jung taught that certain symbols have become ingrained to the human psyche or soul and these he called archetypes. These archetypes have over many years effectively become a part of the human mind, so that without any explanation or conscious understanding, we react and respond when we seem them. Their power therefore, is hereditary. By focussing, concentrating or meditating on these archetypal symbols we can influence or programme ourselves, much like we programme a computer. Since in meditation we open our beings on a higher or energy level to receive a greater influx of those Universal forces we have seen are constantly affecting and shaping our lives and conditions, it follows that the symbols we bring to mind in that meditation will influence us to a similarly increased degree.

So when we meditate with the Full Moon we are bringing ourselves to the same level, individually and collectively, with the archetype of the Moon coupled with the energy or life-principle that the Moon has according to its position in relation to the Sun in the Zodiac at that time. We have made ourselves familiar with the meaning of this archetype in the previous chapter. In this way we are bringing ourselves into alignment with the underlying energy of nature, which the Moon gives to us and becoming more closely linked to Nature herself.

In Astrology each of the planets and signs are given a symbol that astrologers use to draw on the birth chart. These may appear to be simply a means of identification but there is in fact good reason for each symbol used. As we have seen, the symbol for the Moon is the shape of the crescent. This is actually how we see the Moon in the sky when it is midway between its New and First Quarter stage. It faces this way then to symbolise the waxing phase of the Moon, because the Moon represents fertility and growth, the waxing Moon being the time when this occurs. The crescent Moon is also associated with the horns of cattle, the colour of the beast being the phase of the Moon to which it relates: white = New, red = Full, black = Dark. The crescent can also be related to the ark, the boat on which Noah and his companions survived the great flood of the Bible - the Moon of course also making its influence felt here!

Thus the crescent symbolises the Moon as it begins a new phase in relation to the Sun as seen from the Earth. The symbol is, in essence, a half-circle. This traditionally represents the spark of Spirit or Divinity within us. This can also represent the mind. The crescent or half circle is of course incomplete. It is therefore likened to the human in need of fulfilment. A symbol often used to represent the Full Moon is the complete circle, which can of course, represent the human spirit fulfilled or complete. The circle is also a traditional symbol for eternity and that which is immortal, as indeed we are.

When we see the Full Moon in the night sky, we see the shape of a circle. This is another symbol that we respond to at the level of the collective unconscious. It represents certain things to which we have a natural and spontaneous response. A circle represents many things. In can represent the circumference of anything, such as the Earth and therefore comes to be symbolic of the Earth or the World. The circle is often taken to be a symbol of the Sun, which as we have seen is central to our Moon meditations. It can also represent perfection, heaven and eternity. From a purely psychological point of view, a square represents the state of the man who has not achieved inner unity, while the circle represents this state of oneness. The principal symbol of Chinese spirituality, the ubiquitous Yin-Yang symbol, uses the circle to great effect and similarly will repay meditation.

By meditating at the time of the Full Moon, the time of the circle, we can see how we can progress to a wholeness within each complete cycle of the Moon. We move within ourselves from being likened to the incomplete, but growing and changing half-circle to a state of completeness, fulfilment and understanding, with the eternal circle of the Full Moon. By seeing this as an ongoing progressive movement we arrive at the symbol of an upward moving spiral that represents our continual and ever lasting path to fulfilment and completeness. The full circle then moves up to higher levels, as indeed do we, through our meditations. These higher levels we will explore when we begin to move into the Aquarian Age.

In the analytical terms of psychology, the Moon is a symbol of the Mother - the mother within each of us and our need for nurturing, caring and that which protects. This is likened to the mythological beliefs about the Moon, often being Mother goddesses, as we know. Psychology teaches us that we have a natural tendency to be the sort of parent our parents were to us.

The Moon-led associations we make from our parents with security and foundation stay with us through our lives. It is only by conscious effort and then some work on our inner selves that we are able to break any negative programming we may have received from our parents - intentionally or not - and become instead the parent we wish to be.

This applies equally to fathers as to mothers, for each is influencing the child in ways they may or may not be aware of. One way in which we can take charge of and subsequently direct the way in which we parent our children is by the process of Full Moon Meditation. Again, as we open to receive greater amounts of the influence or energy from the Moon in these meditations, so do we increase our awareness of all things parental. For women this can also mean an alignment of their fertility cycles with the movement of the Moon, as it can for men too! By doing this, over a period of time we can become aware of the influence the Moon, our symbolic Mother, has on us and use this consciously to 'channel' our nurturing and caring instincts in the best possible way. This can be both to our own children as well as ourselves and our own 'inner child'.

In psychology the mother is seen as representing the feeling side of life. There are two aspects to the mother, the positive and negative, the natural and unnatural. The natural mother teaches by nourishment and the unnatural mother teaches by adversity. These are paralleled with the necessity of mothers to place their child's needs before their own, at its extreme bringing the possibility of resentment and bitterness on the part of the mother, as she neglects and forgets her own needs. These two mothers are seen as early manifestations of the feminine anima, that is later reborn as the young maiden. These three combine to become the three phases of the Moon. The newborn anima as the waxing Moon, the natural mother as the Full Moon and the unnatural mother the waning Moon. To this is then added the resentful, bitter side which becomes the dark Moon. By our meditations with the Moon we are then coming to terms with and coming to know these psychological archetypes, which represent a major step in our transformation to wholeness.

Another teaching of Jung's that finds a home here is that concerning the make up of the individual human soul. Jung used the term psyche to represent the human soul. This to him was the complete function of all our mental processes. Jung split this into two parts - the feminine and masculine, or Anima and Animus respectively. He saw these as the foundation of the structure of the human with the ability to translate information from the deeper levels of our minds to the conscious level. These can be equated with the principles or energy of the Moon and Sun, as explained in 'Astrology and the Moon'. So by meditating with the Full Moon we are connecting with the very structure and framework of our selves and influencing it according to the subject of our meditation. This, as we have just seen, is to bring about wholeness, understanding and fulfilment.

Jung also believed that the physical man contained within him a female counterpart or animus and the physical female contains within her a male counterpart or anima. This means that a man cannot make contact with his own sub-conscious without making some recognition of his feminine self or anima and the woman cannot contact her sub-conscious without recognising her masculine self, or animus.

It is necessary to be in touch with one's subconscious if one is to become truly whole or 'healed' of the (repressed) fears that hold us back. In this way the subconscious can be identified with our old friend the wolf. He begins however, as an enemy, when he personifies those fears, lurking in the shadows and darkest recesses of our minds. It is only when we beckon to him and entice him out of the darkness, by facing up to our fears, admitting our weaknesses and failures, that the wolf becomes familiar to us and a friend.

Many spiritual and other teachings tell us that our journey to enlightenment or union with God is a journey to wholeness - the term holistic has been much used in recent years in this and many other contexts. A central principle to the holistic view of life is that the sum of the parts is greater than the individual whole, a principle we have already met. This can also be applied to the human condition, requiring in Jungian terms, a joining of the masculine and feminine, or anima and animus, to be complete. If the Sun and Moon represent these archetypes for us in the heavens and if these 'planets' and symbols influence us in the ways that we have seen they do, then how much are we able to use them to take giant strides along our path to this wholeness, completion and fulfilment?

In order to do this we need to absorb the energies of the Sun and the Moon at the most propitious times, into the very basic substance of ourselves, in order to shape our Body. Mind and Spirit, that together form our whole or holistic self. To do this we need to be in a state of 'altered consciousness' or meditation. By consciously opening ourselves up to the energies occurring naturally around us in meditation and combining this with visualisation, we can make use of one of the simplest and most profound gifts the Universe is giving us. Some return is asked and this is where the principle of service comes in, to be examined later.

We are viewed as each having a personality mask or persona as Jung called it, which is the aspect of our overall characters that we present to the world. This is not our true self, but that with which we feel comfortable allowing others to see. This is essentially the way in which we experience and respond to the world. The true self is with us from before our birth and after our death. It is what we truly are, as Spirit, or the Divine that resides within us at all times, through tears and laughter, joy and despair.

Our persona can be viewed as our basic identity. As we know, our basic identity is shaped to a great extent by the time of our birth and the sign of the Zodiac under which we are born. This determines what 'sign' we are and therefore the very basic personality our persona will assume for this lifetime. The Sun was viewed in ancient times as being a masculine symbol and force, and this was balanced and given form and expression by the Moon, seen as a feminine force or power. Once we have the basic personality type, it is then given expression by the force or energy of the Moon. Just as the Sun's influence is divided into twelve 'categories' so the Moon is divided into four phases or influences. Each of these gives its own particular expression and forms the particular influence of the Sun that is prevalent at that time. What this means psychologically is that our personality is being shaped and influenced by the Sun and the Moon, the one giving it form, the other expression.

We will look at other aspects of these four phases in the next chapter, but we will see those influences now from a psychological perspective. The first phase is the Waxing Moon which is identified with the developing personality, when we draw things towards us. This is when we see how things effect only us and respond accordingly, how we see fit. The second phase is the influence of the Full Moon, which is the developed or mature personality, when we see the results of who we are. We are now able to express what we know fully and in a complete way. The third phase is the Waning Moon, the extrovert personality, when we learn from the experience of development. Now we share with others and have a more holistic outlook. The fourth phase is the Dark Moon, the introverted personality, when we nurture our potential, ignore the world and turn inward. We have more regard for the well-being of the whole now and have a spiritual emphasis.

We can see then that these four phases affect the self that we present to the World, and we now know that the Moon is constantly changing us, shaping who we think we are. One way to observe these changes and to use them to a positive effect is by the use of a diary. Perhaps with the use of a notebook or a 'page-a-day' diary, we can record days when we get ideas, when we make plans, when things begin to happen, when we meet obstacles, when things come to fruition and are completed, when we learn, when we help others and so on. You will find that all these things that affect who we are and the way in which we live our lives and more besides, are shaped and directed by the phase of the Moon.

One suggestion for beginning the Full Moon Meditation is to breathe in circles. This simply means to fall into a natural rhythm with your breathing and to continue breathing in circles, by breathing in and out in one fluid movement. Whilst doing this it is possible then to visualise the Full Moon in the sky. By doing this we make the psychological link with the Moon and as we are breathing in circular movements we also make that link on a deeper level, as breathing is an instinctive thing, part of our basic requirement to live.

The collective unconscious as well as the individual subconscious also plays a part in our Dreams. Dreams have been looked on by Jung and subsequent others as a means by which the relevance of symbolic material can be assessed by the individual. Dreams can be looked at as symbolic stories, a series of symbols that our minds create so that we can establish what we feel are appropriate responses to given situations, people etc. Dreams come from our subconscious level, where the Moon also makes its presence felt.

As we know, the Moon moves in cycles. We too are cyclic beings, as physiologically we change according to the level of sunlight available. Babies begin life in an hourly cycle, but adapt to their own families' cycle of sleeping when it is dark and waking when it is light. This is known as the 'circadian rhythm'. It is the cerebral cortex, the part of the brain known as the 'grey matter' that controls these instinctive responses within our bodies. Therefore when daylight begins our bodies chemically change and adjust during the day according to levels of light as well as temperature.

Beyond and literally above this, the actual levels of chemical fluid released by the body to respond accordingly to light and temperature can be seen as being controlled by the phase of the Moon, as we saw in 'The Moon and us'. We can then see how the Moon affects our dreams and these too, move in accordance with the phase of the Moon. By keeping a diary of our dreams and comparing this with the phase of the Moon it is possible for each individual to establish exactly what effect each phase of the Moon has upon them and their dreams.

This is another way in which the deepest contents of our mind, until now unknown to us and a mystery, can be brought to light. So this is also another method by which we can find the courage necessary to face the wolf within us and encourage it to venture nearer to us, to accept food and nourishment and reveal its secrets to us, so that we both may grow.

In our journey now, we emerge back on to the surface of the Moon, where we must rest and recover from our strenuous journey through the darkness within. As we rest we become acclimatised to the atmosphere of the Moon and so observe the different phases it passes through.

8. THE PHASES OF THE MOON

In this chapter we will look at the different phases of the Moon and see how each of these affects us. We will linger long enough on the Moon to discover these things for ourselves, for as we know, it is individual experience that is the key to understanding.

We have already met the two Tarot cards the Magician and the High Priestess, personifying the outer and inner aspects of the basic human nature respectively. We can draw a parallel of these two aspects with the Full and the New Moon respectively. We have already seen how the numbers of these two cards, 1 and 2, can be taken as representing the male and female polarities and it is perhaps these influences we are experiencing when the Moon is at its full and new phase. It has been suggested that the number 2 was formed from the crescent shape of the Moon. We can see when we add our knowledge from the previous chapter that these incoming energies and influences from the Moon speak directly to and effect our animus and anima.

The Full Moon is then taken as affecting and giving us the opportunity to work with the outer, masculine aspect of ourselves, and the New Moon the inner or feminine aspect. As the outer aspect, the Magician and Full Moon represents that which we can present and give to the world, emphasising the healing work that can be done at this time. The New Moon can then be its equal and opposite, when we can take those energies within ourselves. Of course there are aspects of each within the other, just like the ubiquitous black and white Eastern symbol of the Yin/Yang.

If the Full Moon is a time of completion and fulfilment, when things are brought to a head, then the New Moon is the complementary opposite of that - the time when things are begun and things are renewed - from the unknown, dark phase of the Moon. When joined together, these two principles, energies and numbers produce a third principle that is greater than their combination. In other words, 1 + 2 = 3! In Numerology, the number three is the number for creativity, the produce and the child of 1 and 2.

If we return for a moment to the Tarot we can realise that this process is echoed here too. Card number 3 in the sequence of the Major Arcana is the Empress. She is the embodiment of Mother Earth, all that is giving and creative, acting for the good of all who live with her. The combination of experiences of the Magician and the High Priestess results in the Empress, who we are able to work with and aid in her task, that of caring for the planet. We do this by playing our part fully and accepting the responsibility of living with respect and care upon the body of the Earth - Mother Earth herself.

This is the result of our meditations and activities at both the New and Full Moon. This is the new identity we discover, the new feeling and alignment with the wider Universe around us that gives us the inner peace that comes from knowing we are on the right path in our lives and is that which enables us to move more quickly and accurately to the centre of the Universe that is the ultimate goal of us all.

We can see this process as taking control of our lives, or taking charge of our fate, a natural by-product of meditation that can be capitalised on by meditating at the time of the New and Full Moon. As we have seen these are the times of most significance to us so we are therefore able to benefit most from them. In legend, there are three Fates, These are Clotho, who spins the thread of life, like the New Moon, Lachesis who measures the length of the thread of life with her staff, like the Full Moon and Atropos, who cuts the thread of life short with her shears, like the crone of the dark Moon. Thus we are able to, quite literally, take control of fate, by facing and merging with the energy of the New and Full Moon and allowing it to flow through and change us and adapting ourselves accordingly as we go.

The New Moon then is the time when things are begun. This can be plans, ideas, practical projects, interests, hobbies, relationships - in fact anything in our lives. It is not however, limited to that which is within our lives. It is also without us. That is, it is a time when the natural energies are being regenerated and renewed around us. We have already seen that the energy of each Full Moon is dependent upon which sign of the Zodiac the Sun is in - where it is in our sky. At the Full Moon meditation we focus on those energies and principles as they are working practically in our lives - outside of our bodies and minds. To do this to the maximum potential we need to first absorb the particular energy of each cycle of the Moon. We need to open Body, Mind and Spirit to the natural energy the Universe is emanating at that time. This is the function of the New Moon meditation. It is the inner preparation for the successful fulfilment of the work that we do at Full Moon. It should be seen as equal in every way to the Full Moon. It is the feminine 'complementary opposite' of the masculine Full Moon.

So if the Full Moon Meditation is seen as focussing and assimilating the light of the Sun, the masculine planet and principle, the New Moon Meditation is the time to balance that and allow the direct and mysterious feel and flow of the feminine Moon into our systems. In this way we are able to attune ourselves to the natural tides within our bodies of ebb and flow, just as the tides of the oceans and seas ebb and flow.

There is a Universal rhythm to these tides. By meditating at the time of the New and Full Moon we are moving in time with the rhythm of the Universe. If the Moon is seen as the mediator between our inner selves and the outer world then it follows that we must allow its influence inside us before we can direct it to have an effect in our lives.

Meditation at the time of the New Moon is then a valuable tool for giving ourselves the inherent balance that exists within the Universe, within ourselves. It may not be as universally recognised as being as important as the Full Moon, but as we have seen it serves a vital purpose.

It will be found that meditation at the time of the New Moon provides a bridge for adjusting out of the internal and contemplative phase of the Dark Moon and into the newness and freshness of the New Moon. Hold this purpose in mind during your daily meditation, to allow this energy to flow through you and recognise its signs in your outer life.

As the New Moon heralds a time of action rather than contemplation it is a good thing to celebrate this in an active way. This can be one simple act that you are aware recognises the shift in Universal energies or it could perhaps be a circle or sacred dance, or full ritual designed specifically to reflect the particular energies of that time and that Moon. Perhaps a simple hug with the person next to you. These are suggestions for you to work on.

We have seen how there are four phases of the Moon to be considered, each with its own particular influence and way in which we can make use of those influences. Each cycle of the Moon is complete in itself and can then be divided into the following four phases. Included with each phase are the influences pertaining to each one that we need to be aware of and can connect with in our daily meditations and activities. In this way we can attune ourselves deeply to what nature is doing and feeling at any given moment. It becomes part of our very essence and self.

Gardening by the phases of the Moon is a traditional and widespread practice that utilises the natural forces and energies of the Moon in a most practical way. The basic principles are that all activities for growth and bringing things to fruition should take place during the waxing phase, with produce for immediate consumption gathered during this phase too. Cutting of plants etc. should be done during the waning Moon, along with harvesting, and planting root crops.

It is also worth mentioning here that just as the Moon reflects the light of the Sun, so the Sun has four phases which can be compared to the Moon. These four phases are actually on two levels. Firstly, the cycle of the Sun through a day or twenty-four hours, split into times of Dawn, Noon, Dusk and Night. Secondly, the cycle of the Sun through the year, central to the beliefs and customs of so many ancient peoples. Here the phases of the Sun are the seasons of Spring, Summer, Autumn and Winter. Together, the interplay of the Sun and Moon represent the interaction of the male and female and the forces or polarities of each, making a parallel with the full and New Moon phases.

WAXING MOON

This is regarded as the Planting Time, so is the time to sow seeds of new ideas, plans, thoughts, words and actions. In short to change, in however apparently small a way, our very beings. Ideas can often begin and take root now in our subconscious minds, where we need to make some effort, such as by meditation, to become aware of their content. Things that we notice and affect us often reside in our subconscious, to be accessed and brought up to the level of our conscious mind at the appropriate time, just as we now call up or access a particular file on a computer. We can then open this file, take out the appropriate and useful information at that time and either discard the rest or file it away again, to be reused at a later date. The time around the New Moon, the beginning of the waxing or growing phase, is the time to do this, when we will find it easier to face and use the contents of our subconscious. In our meditations we can ask for help with our deeds and especially any new projects etc. that we are starting.

On a global level we can direct energy to places that are beginning new phases of direction, of which there seem to be many at this time. Another aspect of the influence of the New Moon is that of having a youthful outlook in the way that we are and approach our lives. The energies coming to us from the Moon at this time are particularly suited to the optimism and surety of youth. The New Moon is likened to the Sun at Dawn, the bringer of life and the hope and renewal of the day's light. The New Moon is also compared to the season of Spring, the time when new shoots emerge and hope is renewed for the warmth and light return to the sky and our bodies. This is the time of preparation for what lies ahead, on two levels.

Firstly the microcosmic level of each lunar month, when we prepare for our plans and activities etc. during the time until the Full Moon and secondly the macrocosmic level. This is when we look further ahead and see the renewal that is happening at a deeper level within ourselves, as we develop and grow over the years to the fulfilment of our potential and, we hope, our destiny. This is a time to bring the New Moon energies down into ourselves and ensure that what we asked for at that time becomes real and is not allowed to drift away. We need to generate more power to the energy we have created by our awareness and thoughts from the time of the New Moon to keep the flow going and increasing.

We can do this by attuning to our own needs as the Moon increases and sends the energy to us. We need to nourish ourselves with thoughts and meditations to this effect and thus regenerate our bodies and selves in the correct way. We can then express ourselves in the correct way and allow the individual and unique powers that we do have, given by the Universe and related into a form which we can use by the Moon, to flourish and provide us with all that we need and more, enabling us to help those in need.

We all have creative powers in one form or another and this is the time to allow them expression. If they are not recognised as such, this does not change the reality of their existence and so it does not matter. The energies of the Moon are fast-flowing now and so we are able to make things work, using physical effort and mental application. We should overcome any obstacles in this phase and continue with working hard toward our goals, keeping things in a real perspective. The Moon now is larger and makes a 'D' shape in the sky, by which we can recognise this phase. The crescent of the New Moon has expanded and brings with it the promise of the complete circle of the Full Moon. The Sun and Moon are at right angles to each other at the time of the First Quarter with the Moon in the West during the first half of the night. This is a yin influence becoming yang, for those who are versed in these Eastern terms and ways.

Psychologically the Waxing phase of the Moon is looked upon as the extrovert phase, since it is growing and giving out. Our natural tendencies will therefore incline to being more extrovert. Magically our workings during this phase should be to give out, to heal others and to work with anything that is increasing.

There are colours associated with the phases of the Moon too, linked with the Triple Goddess and her three faces. The New Moon or maiden aspect of the goddess has the colour white, to link with purity, innocence and the virginity she possesses. It is also said to be the white of the imagination, a blank sheet from which ideas will spring to be coloured. In our workings and meditations we can then use white as appropriate, whether to cover the altar or to burn white candles.

FULL MOON

This is the time when, as we know we are most affected by the Moon and when its powers are at their height. This is the time when we can fulfil our dreams, wishes, hopes and desires. Now we can invoke and pull down the energies of the Moon directly into ourselves and our lives and direct them with loving intent to others in need. Of course if we too are in need of these qualities of light, love and healing, then we can attract these to our lives now. Abundance can be ours, in terms of love and friendship, humanity and cooperation with the rest of the world. Thus our thoughts directed through meditation are especially effective now.

This is the time when our personalities can be developed and our outer characters can be shaped and progressed as we would wish. Our individuality shows itself now in the way we are and we can freely express our true selves. The Sun and Moon are opposite each other at this time, so, cloud permitting, the surface of the Moon is lit to enable us to see the complete circle.

The time of the Full Moon is likened to Noon with the Sun at its height, physically and energetically, of its power, just as with the Moon. This can also be compared to the season of Summer, when again the Sun has a stronger heat to give us and more time to do it in, as it is closer to us. This is a yang influence.

In psychology, we would consider this to be the maternal aspect, as the Full Moon is closely linked to the Mother aspect of the goddess. So our natural tendencies are for nurturing, caring and sharing, as well as an awareness of fertility and reproduction. From this the colour of the Full Moon is red, in part due to the blood of menstruating women at this time. Red is also used traditionally to represent activity and action, and is an energising colour, used to stimulate and revive.

WANING MOON

This is the time when the peak has been reached and things begin to quieten down and flow away from us. Thus it is a time to help others in whatever way is practical and to give of ourselves to what and who is around us. In our meditations we can continue to radiate the qualities we invoked at the Full Moon in the knowledge that the phase of the Moon is especially suited and will magnetically assist the flow of our thoughts and energy to where it is directed and needed.

The Last Quarter is a time of healing and for looking deep within ourselves to learn wisdom, that we each have within. We can both teach and learn now, from within ourselves and from and to others. The energy of the Moon is especially suited to the flow of thought and word from one to another, both in a practical and a meditative way. The Moon is decreasing in size and shape, just as the energies flow away from us. The Sun and Moon are once again at right angles to each other and the Moon is seen in the East. In the cycle of the daily movement of the Sun, the waning Moon is likened to the time of Dusk, when the light and warmth departs and we come to rest and turn inward. This is the same as the season of Autumn, when we gather in the harvest and settle down later to rest and renewal. This is a yang influence becoming yin.

Psychologically we have tendencies towards introversion, when we will wish to be still and contemplative, tendencies which we can easily utilise in daily meditation. The energies and impulses we receive from the Moon during the waning phase slow us down and cause us to need a little more rest. Magically this is the time to banish and be rid of that which is not productive, to do otherwise is literally to go against the tide. We will find also that communication between loved ones becomes more intimate, as secrets are apt to be shared with those we trust.

DARK MOON

The dark of the Moon lasts for approximately four days and was regarded with great suspicion in olden times, as the Goddess was thought to have turned her face, and her blessing, away from the people. It is now a time of inner, silent work, when our dreams may well affect us strongly. We can use these to gain new insights as to what is required for the next phase.

This is a time of rest and repose, when the energies seem to flow to the centre of our beings, quietening and calming us. Now symbolically we die and are reborn, just as the Moon disappears from view to emerge again later as the crescent of the New Moon once more. The Moon is not visible and we must simply be still and pray for its return. It rises in almost the same direction as the Sun, which thus does not illuminate its surface. This is the time of Night when the Sun is not visible to us and appears to have died, with all being quiet. Of course it brings with it the promise of its return and the new day, just as with the turn of the season at Mid-Winter we begin to look for the lengthening of the light of the day and the promise of the return of Spring. In the meantime however, all is quiet and calm, whilst we withdraw and regenerate. This is a yin influence.

The Dark Moon is the province of the Crone or hag aspect of the Moon goddess, the haggard looking old woman whose ways and words are a mystery to us, unless she chooses to explain herself. This is her choice and privilege, which she has earned by her work and experience through the years. We must sit and wait patiently, treating her with the respect that is her due. This is a time of silence and occasional depression, as we sink to the very depths of our soul. It takes some wisdom and experience to fully understand the role of this aspect of our personalities, but if we are gentle and patient these things will be revealed to us.

The creative personality frequently identifies with this aspect. True creative souls are renowned for being unstable emotionally, or when viewed by the unknowing and uncompassionate, crazy. This wild process is all part of their creativity however, for it is precisely from out of the ashes of these black depressions that ideas and inspirations spring. The old woman is strange, but wise. It is from these times that truly great music is composed and pictures created, We must be truly thankful for the suffering and trials of those bittersweet souls who must endure the ravages of their own particular wolves. History shows us that many of the greatest composers, such as Beethoven and Mozart in the classical field, or in a different way and field and more recently, Vincent Van Gogh and Eric Clapton, did the things they did out of battling with their own particular inner struggle and torment. Indeed it is said that any true blues musician must be suffering within to truly know and express the blues through their music.

The colour of this particular aspect of the Moon's phases is then black, like the depths of the night. The darkest hour is however, just before dawn, and if we are still long enough we will begin to see the first grey streaks of dawn, before its bright white brilliance shines once more. We can then catch sight of the crescent Moon in the sky, as we return full circle to the New Moon again. The goddess is reborn as the maiden and a new mystery is born.

So we can see the natural and beautiful flow of forces emanating from the Moon during a complete cycle from new to full, and back to new again. In this many mysteries are explained and things revealed. Above all, we are able to reveal these things from within ourselves.

Having lingered on the surface of the Moon, we must now turn our eyes to the future, to consider the consequences of our actions, consulting the crystal ball and waiting for the mists to clear to reveal to us what lies ahead.

9. THE AQUARIAN AGE

At this stage in our study we will take a look ahead, at the coming Aquarian Age and its effect upon humanity. We will discover through this that Full Moon Meditation can play a vital part in aiding the transition from this present age to the new or Aquarian Age.

The term the Aquarian Age is often dubbed the 'New Age'. This is somewhat misleading and has come to be associated with traits that have nothing to do with our purpose here, namely the rampant spread of commercialism and 'pie in the sky' theories and methods. Many people today, with good reason as we shall see, have turned to false and surface ideas and methods of spirituality. The result of many such theories is to leave the participant in a rosy world where the pretence is that all is wonderful and all things will naturally work out as God intended. This may be so, but while we still have famine, war, rape and torture in our world, there is a great part we can play to help alleviate the suffering of those many individuals.

Esoteric teaching tells us that humanity moves through periods or stages in its history, called ages, and that each of these ages is linked to the properties of the signs of the Zodiac. We have, until now, been living in the age of Pisces, the time of Christ. Depending on which source you read, the years between approximately 1987 to 2040 are a transition period when we move from the old age to the new age, from the Piscean to the Aquarian Age.

This Aquarian Age then carries with it the properties and characteristics associated with the sign of Aquarius in the zodiac. This means that the energies and influences that emanate to us from the Divine, from the Universe, above and all around us, are of the particular type that those born under the sign of Aquarius will be familiar with.

Aquarians then are communicative sorts with a high degree of self expression at their disposal. They are spontaneous people, giving them strong intuition and are often unconventional. They are progressive, often linking themselves with the forward thinking aims of the community. Mentally they are very active and can be intense. Humanitarianism is high on their agenda, giving them an ability to use their communicative skills for agreements and synthesis with others. Their faults can be in dogmatism and eccentricity and at the extreme can lack integrity and lose their principles.

Translated to a global level, this means that humanity is being given the opportunity to use the energies that are being given to it through the Aquarian Age to align with each other, to seek common goals, of synthesis and progression, in its society and community.

The use of intuition can be relied upon far more consciously than at present and the mind can be used for new ideas. We can come to recognise the sanctity of all life and find a new freedom for each individual. We must lose all dogma and retain the highest of integrity and ethics. We can see some of these things happening on a small scale in some places now, but obviously there is a great deal to be done if these grand words are to become reality.

We must recognise our duty, as part of our spiritual service, to assist this transition in the best way we can, in these times. One such way is the practice of working with the Moon in the ways outlined here. There are many other such ways, each of which can be tested and verified by its practicality and effectiveness in the real world, rather than its comfort and ease of operation, or by being surrounded by a guru who gives you truth. Truth you must discover for yourself, from within. Then apply that truth to your practical life and you will be fulfilling your destiny.

We may justifiably ask what are the sources of such teaching and what is this 'Esoteric teaching'. For our answer, we will look to the works of Alice Bailey and the Tibetan. Many works were and are published by the Lucis Trust (see Bibliography) by the author Alice Bailey who committed to paper a great deal of information and teaching pertaining to the Aquarian Age.

Written many years before they became accepted and popular, in the early to mid 1900's, these teachings are now required reading for any who choose to fully understand what is happening to humanity and the world upon which it lives. I would refer readers to the statement from the Tibetan that precedes each of these works for verification as to their depth, wisdom and spiritual authority.

The Tibetan, as he calls himself, is a discarnate entity, a spirit who no longer lives in a physical body on the earth, who was able to communicate through Alice Bailey. In recent years we have seen a veritable explosion of this phenomena, now called 'channelling' This has been met with much derision in some quarters and rightly so, for there is sadly much rubbish written. There is also much wisdom and material that is of use, in which category must fall the works of the Tibetan, "a disciple of a certain degree".

In the work entitled '*Glamour, A World Problem*' the Tibetan says "I ask therefore, for your service ... and I request that you give increased attention at the time of the Full Moon'. Later in the same text he exhorts us to "work along the line of dispelling glamour at the Full Moon". Just why he should say that the Full Moon needs increased attention we have already seen, so this brings us to an explanation of service.

As I have mentioned before, part of our work with the Full Moon is to perform our required spiritual service. Spiritual and esoteric teachings the world over agree that we cannot progress spiritually by satisfying the needs of the flesh alone or the mind or ego. This is why the Tibetan tells us to dispel glamour; the glamour of the ego, which is an illusion. Rather the wisdom, knowledge and awareness that we gain along our path is to be used for the benefit of others, to help the progress of humanity as a whole and to assist the unfoldment of the 'great plan'. In this way we serve, both other people, the planet and the whole Universe, or if you prefer, 'God' or the Divine. It is through such selfless service that we can truly progress.

There are many ways to provide this service, some practical, some dealing with more ethereal levels. Both are essential and need each other. Full Moon Meditation falls into the ethereal category and works by the distribution of energies to help those people, places and situations that are in need at any one time. In this way we dispel glamour and illusion and serve others.

In the book "*Esoteric Healing*", Alice Bailey also states that we can get a "more harmonious distribution of force for the benefit of all", exemplifying in this the way of service outlined above. So as to be absolutely clear that our motives in working with the Moon cannot be for self aggrandisement or gain, the Tibetan, through Alice Bailey, then states that we need to "clear the field of the personality so that the higher energies can have freer play". It is necessary then to remove any personal bias or emotion during our meditations, as far as is possible.

This book then goes on to explain that it is this state of harmony within, necessary for the optimum effect of our meditation, that allows for the state of harmony without, in the wider world, that is its result. This harmony can be established regardless of what personal trauma or emotion we might be suffering, through a process I call Grounding and Connecting, explained in Chapter 11. This enables us to be free of selfish thought and so, following the principle that energy follows thought, deed. It is not simply a case of thinking about one's fellow humans for the time of the meditation, but living one's life in such a way as to know the suffering humanity has as a whole and feeling this as a part of our own being. For as the Biblical Paul said, we are truly "Members one of another".

When we recognise this relationship we view life through different eyes. The actions of those who would seek to make a fast buck out of those more vulnerable than themselves and many such others, can be viewed with compassion, for it can be seen that they are only done because of that individual or group of people's, weakness and lack of understanding. Really, these things are likely to continue, until the majority of those alive at any one time are able to grasp these things and experience this fact for themselves. Then, and perhaps only then, can we be said to be living in the Aquarian Age. Until that time, we must continue to do our bit, not with the faith, but the knowledge that we each must do this, if humanity is to fulfil its potential and we are to survive on this planet in its present form.

In the book "*Esoteric Healing*" the Tibetan tells us that "the mystery of the Moon is the mystery of failure" and that the energy coming from the Moon contains the "seeds of death and disease". Spoken in the context of the unknown part of ourselves and the mystery of the Moon which in this book I hope to have gone some way to reveal, these words remind us of the result of ignoring the above principles and effects. To be ignorant of the law in our land is not an excuse for breaking it and it is so with esoteric law too.

Esoterically, the energies flow from the Moon whether we are aware of them or not and whether we believe in them or not, as surely as night follows day. To consciously choose to ignore them is take the responsibility for oneself, that is each person's choice. But to simply live your life attempting to cosset yourself away from such basic truths as the wheel of nature through the year and the effect this has upon us, is to live a lie. This is to accept defeat without fighting, to never even admit one has fears, let alone face them. The wolf is given free reign and is allowed to devour the soul without restraint. Thus the death and disease the Tibetan speaks of is also allowed free reign, the mystery of the Moon remains just that and we are subject to the fear of death and the misery of disease. Of course, by consciously working with and transforming those energies we can bring life where there was death and healing where there was disease, through understanding. This is each and every persons choice as we enter the Aquarian Age.

Through this process as we know, the wolf becomes the dog, tame and friendly and our loyal ally. This happens on a global as well as individual level, when we include the principles of the shift into the Aquarian Age. Collectively we are in a time of great potential when humanity is presented with an opportunity to bring peace to its world and a new understanding to its inhabitants. We are able to make great advances as a civilisation at this time.

"*Esoteric Healing*" also includes some indications that we cannot allow our fears to conquer us and the wolf to roam free and wild within, lest we succumb to the entrancement of the Moon and our howls of pain and anguish be heard in the night. The book speaks of "lunar lords", who are "those who work under the control of the Moon". These forces are linked to what the Tibetan calls the "lower personality", that is our selfish thoughts and emotions, the physical and mental senses. To satisfy only these brings disease, ill health and death. the principle is obviously not that we cannot have physical and mental pleasure, but these cannot become our guiding lights and goals. Remember, you must make your choice.

To provide further help to enable you to make your choice (though by reading this book perhaps you are demonstrating your choice is made!) we can look further at this remarkable book "Esoteric Healing". Knowing that working with the Full Moon can give us a harmony within and a degree of inner balance and peace we have not known before, the book tells us that the period of the Full Moon can have a quite definite effect on unbalanced people.

The Tibetan explains that there are three reasons that the neuroses present within people are so prevelant through the period of the Full Moon. The first of these is due to this transition between the ages of Pisces and Aquarius and the change in energies this brings. The Tibetan tells us that this is like changing from living on earth to living in water. It is a change in the medium through which we move and have our being. The very stuff of life has changed and we must flow and change with it. The principle is the same as that of the Full Moon. We have already seen how at this time greater amounts of energy and force come from the Moon down to the Earth, affecting all. This brings up to the surface what is naturally below, be it balance, peace and harmony or wildness, tension and imbalance - or in other words a wild wolf or a tame dog.

Since one of the basic principles of the Aquarian Age is humanity, together with the collapse of old ways and the formation of a new society, it follows that we must allow ourselves to change as these new energies come to us. This is the second reason for the Moon adversely affecting some people, a lack of fluidity and ability to change. The Tibetan tells us that higher spiritual beings are bringing about energies that allow for a collapse to old outmoded forms and the construction of new ones. This is happening across the world, with many countries changing, some peacefully, some through war and bloodshed. How is it in your own heart?

The last reason given by the Tibetan for the affliction of the Moon is that more light and energy is able to come from the astral plane or level. This is the realm in which, as previously explained, energy forms into reality. This is where the energy in 'energy follows thought' resides, or quite literally 'hangs out'! As more light flows down, so those who are sensitive to such energies respond instinctively and without direction or focus. We are told that we need to adjust to the light.

To me this means that we need to 'channel' those energies through us, the same as a lightning rod channels the electricity or energy from a lightning bolt down the side of a building and into the Earth rather than through the inhabitants of the building, frying them in the process! We each need to earth or ground this energy as it naturally flows through us, keeping us in touch with reality and denying the control of the soul. It often seems, on looking round many 'new age' shops and groups that there is much work to be done!

We have looked at just one of the sources of 'channelled' material available today, albeit a reputable and respected one. By way of example, we will look briefly at another such source, that channelled by a group of people and calling itself 'Ramala'. These teachings state that the "primary purpose of the Moon is to lead Humanity into a greater understanding of the Cosmos (which means 'beautiful order' - or can be called the Universe).

They go on to explain that the relationship between the Earth and the Moon in effect contains the secret to creation in the Universe. The Moon is seen as having a vital part to play in the spiritual destiny of the Earth, being its satellite. The *Revelation of Ramala* also states that the Moon is also the key to Humanity's "development beyond the Moon". We are told therein to reach upward and search for ourselves for this secret - perhaps in our Full Moon meditation this is what we are attempting to do. The secret that the wild wolf holds over us.

Ramala goes on to explain that just as we have four seasons, races, points of the compass and so on, so does the Moon have four phases - the New/Waxing, Full, Waning and Dark that we have dealt with. Each of these four phases of the Moon corresponds to the four Kingdoms of Matter on the Earth - Animal, Mineral, Vegetable and Water/Human - remembering that we are "bags of mostly water".

In particular, Ramala teaches us that the Moon influences the pineal gland, which is the "learning gland of humanity" which controls our knowledge and inspiration. So at the time of the Full Moon when its power is greatest so are our powers of receptivity. By opening ourselves still further in meditation at the time of the

Full Moon, we are opening ourselves to learn from the Moon's influence and so are able to help humanities progress and transition to the Aquarian Age. We can then perform our service in this way to much greater effect.

There are many other such sources of higher wisdom available, each with its own interpretation and way of looking at the world. I would simply add a reminder here, when you are reading such material to always apply discretion and intuition. Do not be afraid to discount teaching, just because it purports to come from some high source or another.

Here then we have cast our eyes into the future a little, to examine the likely and possible effects of our Full Moon Meditations. We have seen much and I hope understood a little more of why we participate in this practice. We must remember not to become captivated by the view we have ahead of us however, and must remember that we live in an ever lasting present that is our only reality. It is in this reality that we must do our work, involving blood, sweat and even tears. What are these compared to the rewards on offer?

Through our studies we have come to realise that the time of the Full Moon is a time special in our development and at this stage in humanities history, an opportunity to assist in the making and dawning of a new age. It is then, a celebration, of the knowledge and reality of the spiritual, immortal being within all of us and of the acknowledgment of a specific time in the dance in the heavens which for so long has inspired so many people in so many ways. Let us now prepare for that celebration.

10. THE FULL MOON

Any meditation, ritual or celebration of any kind needs preparation for its successful outworking and Full Moon Meditation is no exception. In this chapter we will look at the Full Moon itself and expose ourselves to the full glare and light of the Goddess in this way. We will also prepare ourselves for our work of service.

There are two cycles of the Full Moon which we must look at here. The first is that of the five day cycle to each Full Moon phase and the second is that of the annual cycle or rhythm. We know already that each Full Moon emits a particular nature or type of energy to us, dependent upon the position of the Sun in a certain sign of the Zodiac, remembering that the Moon reflects the light of the Sun. Over and above this, there is also a series of Full Moon's that occurs at a certain time of the year, for a period of three months, or Moon's.

We must begin our preparation by knowing that the period of the Full Moon actually lasts for five days (or nights). Although there is an accurately pinpointed moment in time when the Moon reaches the stage in its journey where it is absolutely opposite the Sun, thus appearing full to us on Earth, in terms of its influence and energy, we receive the influence of the Full Moon for five days. This complies with the known effect of this period on mental patients and the like.

This five day period has to it a definite cycle, that leads up to a point of climax or maximum activity, as regards the Moon's influence upon us, on the middle day of the five. When working with the Moon in this way, we can use the two days preceding the 'full day' to be gathering those energies from the Moon to ourself, to be homing in to the needs of those we know, those we don't and the places on our planet that we see are in difficulty at this time. These things can be done by concentrating on them during our daily meditation, and individually prior to group meeting. When we then come to meet together on the day of the Full Moon or as near as is practically possible, we are prepared in the best way possible to invoke and release an optimum amount of healing energy to those in need. The remaining two days are again for individual work, this time focussing on continuing to distribute that radiation of energy. With tongue very firmly in cheek, we could recall here the famous words of Timothy Leary in the 1960's, when he told us to "Turn On, Tune In and Drop Out", but used in a somewhat different context!

These five days of the Full Moon also come to us from accepted esoteric teaching, again that of the Tibetan through Alice Bailey. As we know at this time we receive more reflected light from the Sun. We know that because of this we can meditate to a deeper degree and with a correspondingly deeper and stronger result and effect. The conditions for meditation are at their optimum, courtesy of the Goddess, when the Moon is full. It seems almost a crime not to utilise this gift in some way.

In "The Reappearance of the Christ", the Tibetan tells us that we can strengthen our spirit of invocation and multiply the influences that we evoke. These qualities of invocation and evocation can be aligned to the days before and after the day of the Full Moon respectively. This same book goes on to explain that it is by the power of thought, focussed and directed, that we can create an "outgoing stream of energy".

As all things on our Earthly plane and level have their reflection on the higher levels and planes, so does the five day rhythm of the Full Moon have its reflection over an annual period too. This occurs over the Moon's that are Full while the

Sun is in the signs of Aries, Taurus and Gemini, which occur around April, May and June respectively. These Full Moon's can represent the culmination of the year's work with the Moon, for they each have special qualities that can be aligned to the five day rhythm.

The first of these three Moon's is the Aries Moon, often also known as the Easter or Christ Festival, for it falls around this time, the time of Easter of course being set each year by the Full Moon preceding it. This is the "expression of the love of God" and a time when in our meditation we can invoke this, to gather it to us, readying ourselves for the great work of distributing it to the wider world. Of course as you do this you are highly liable to feel it flow through you as well. Over the month of this Moon (from New through Full to New) you can, in your daily meditations, be attuning yourself to the problems and need for love and healing that exist in the planet. This should not be a problem - there are many! View them all with love and compassion, as did Christ.

This then culminates in the Festival of Wesak, the Taurus Moon, around May. This is also known as the Festival of Buddha for it is said to fall on the Buddhas birthday. The Tibetan tells us that Buddha was the "intermediary between the highest spiritual centre". This time we can experience the "expression of the wisdom of God", the meaning of which I will leave for you to discover through your own meditations. Here we focus on the divine purpose of the energy we have invoked, namely to give love, healing and life to all. By this we create a vessel of ourselves and our groups, ready to allow the energy to flow out with the next Moon. Through this month there is an intense period of work to store this energy and become fully aware of its purpose.

Next comes the blessed release, with the Festival of Goodwill, the Full Moon of Gemini, also known as World Invocation Day or the Festival of Humanity. Now we can distribute and radiate out the force we have created. At this time the spiritual and divine nature of humanity is recognised. We are exhorted to aspire towards Godhood and to seek "conformity with the will of God" in our own daily meditation. This is the time of the work of both the Buddha and the Christ. This is a time for unity and togetherness, when the joy of celebrating together can be expressed.

If you need any further convincing that this work is important, the Tibetan also tells us that as humanity invokes this power, the spiritual hierarchy, the otherworldly order of beings who shape the physical reality we have, are empowered to carry out Gods plan on Earth. So when you meditate with the Full Moon's in his way, you are readily helping the Universe to manifest the way it should. As we know, this is done by the 'energy follows thought' principle, so that as together we send out similarly aligned thoughts at the same time i.e. the time of the Full Moon, so they join together, being compatible and create physical reality.

So it is our concentration and will that emits the strength of the life force and energy that we are able to send to others. We are told that this energy goes first to "spiritual beings" and then to the hearts and minds of men, so we are not only healing the planet, but helping those who share it with us. In the instructions for the meditations given in the next chapter, you will see that a time is spent on focussing upon the highest source of energy and light, so as to bring this down to a level where we can hold and distribute it. Bringing this down to the necessary level can be quite a strain, especially when a group has been formed and established for a time and may give rise to some pressure about the head and even discomfort. My simple answer to this is that this is a terribly small price to pay for helping to heal the planet and forms part of your work of service anyway. You are really being blessed for the work you are doing.

The Tibetan explains in "*Esoteric Healing*" that those who are unbalanced, are unbalanced in energy and so suffer the affliction of being upset with hallucinations and phobias when the Moon is full. He also explains that those who are "aspirants", those who are in control of their faculties and have a clear and defined conscious desire to grow and serve spiritually, can "profit by these Full Moon cycles". This profit is not a financial one of course, but one of understanding and development and above all, service, from which everything leads. As part of your own individual preparation, I would exhort you to ask of yourself to what do you aspire? When you have arrived at a clear and conscious resolution of your need to serve and know why this is so, then you can begin to reap the rewards. This does not preclude you from participating in Full Moon Meditation of course, for it may be by this process that you discover your answer to this question.

Until such time I would also exhort you to be wary of the effect the Moon is having upon you, especially if you choose to open yourself to receiving her influence through meditation. I say this not to give alarm, but to instill the correct procedures from the outset. The Tibetan tells us that those who are unbalanced are overstimulated are "swept by emotional desire and psychically upset". I do not wish to be the instigator of such things! If an individual gleefully throws themselves into Full Moon Meditation without thought or awareness of what they are really doing, they are asking to be given an overdose of energies, which underlie and form their physical reality, which they could not control or handle. Their lives are if effect then, out of control. This principle applies in many areas of life and is no more than common sense. Who among us would expect to be able to fly an aeroplane without tuition or run a marathon without training?

In another book, *"Glamour, A World Problem"*, the Tibetan tells us to be on the lookout for "undue stimulation" of our emotions and energies when the Moon is full. Whilst instructing us to intensify our efforts at this time, he goes on to say that it is preferable to work as a group rather than individually to ensure that the imbalances spoken of above do not occur. It is clear then that we need to protect ourselves and regulate the flow that we are opening ourselves to, to avoid these pitfalls and potential dangers.

It is necessary to place this protection around you to ensure that you are safe and secure when you open yourself from within to work with energy in the way we have outlined. To leave yourself unprotected is to court disaster. When we work with energy in this way, contacting a force from a higher level, this acts like a light on the higher or astral levels. The force of concentration from a group of people meditating together creates a light on the astral level. This acts like a beacon to attract beings on that level, like (with respect to them) 'moths to a flame'. Some of those beings may be less evolved than others and would seek to lead astray the intentions of those providing it or to simply render ineffective the efforts for good they are trying to have.

The way that you choose to place protection around your group and working area may be dependent on your or your group's beliefs and tradition of workings. For instance a Christian group may pray and directly ask for God's protection. Similarly, if you are working from a particular Pagan perspective or tradition, you may wish to ask the appropriate deities to be present to protect you, whether they be from the Egyptian, Greek, Norse, Celtic or whatever pantheon. Many useful and effective methods of setting up a protective space are given in a great many magical books and I would not presume to offer something that is better than those.

At risk of being accused of sidestepping the issue, but to avoid offending anyone, I will offer my own simple but effective non-denominational method, that I will call the Attunement. For those readers eager to cast a magical circle about themselves and work in this effective and powerful manner, I would suggest consulting the book *'Pathworking'* by Pete Jennings and Pete Sawyer, which includes a suitably non-specific circle casting, based on the Elements of Earth, Air, Fire and Water.

Another aspect of casting this circle is to create a sacred space in which to perform your work, be it ritual, meditation, sacred drama or other celebration. An awareness that you are in a sacred space helps, in the instance of Full Moon Meditation, to give an awareness of the sacredness of the time and the meaning of the event. This is true of course of any other magical or spiritual working, for whatever reason. The Attunement also serves to begin the process of calming each individual and attuning them to the energies of the time and to themselves, the Earth and the wider Universe.

We begin by standing in a circle and joining hands. There is a particular way of doing this that I use, which seems to reveal difficulty amongst my students of deciphering right and left and up and down! I request my students to join hands so that the right hand faces up and the left hand faces down.

As a professional Tarot consultant, I am heavily influenced, as you may have guessed, by the Tarot and its ways. We have already met the Magician and seen something of his nature in these pages. The Magician is usually shown with his right hand raised aloft and his left hand pointing down to the Earth. This can vary, for reasons specific to each Tarot pack. Part of the function of the Magician is to allow himself to be the conductor of energy, or the mediator of this force, similar to our Grounding and Connecting procedure, set out below. He therefore points up with his right hand and down with his left to indicate that he receives this power, not from himself but from above. This travels through him and out his left hand and on into the Earth. He is acknowledging a higher power and force and lets this 'channel' through him. This is what we do in our attunement, so we have the right hand up and the left hand down.

There is no set way to work and this is no more than a foible of mine, with which you are free to disagree. You may like to consider that in traditional healing meditation, the hands are usually positioned so that when one is giving out healing energy, the hands are facing palm upwards on the lap to enable the energy to flow out easier and when not, turned palm down, so as to retain it.

Another reason for my working in the right hand up, left hand down method is that the left side of the body is regarded as the intuitive, instinctive side, corresponding with the right hemisphere of the brain in this. The intuitive nature is more suited to drawing in energy, whilst the rational, logical side, the right side, is more suited to passing it on, which is the method employed when working in this way.

If you can imagine a group of people standing in a circle with hands linked in this way, each distributing energy, the result is that its flow will be anti clockwise around the group. Some people may feel uncomfortable with this and as stated, this can easily be changed to reverse the flow. The effect will be the same if the purpose is kept in mind.

So the process is then to stand and join hands and become relaxed, perhaps by following a particular breathing pattern. I have found that simply counting your breath to the rhythm of four in and four out achieves this. This is a traditional way of working, where the rhythm of four is conducive to relaxation, so the time which it takes you to count to four is not so important.

Having become relaxed, you are then able to let your senses become aware of the energy and atmosphere in the place you are in. Then visualise this energy as a golden stream of clear light. Direct this with your thought and concentration down your right arm and out through the palm of your right hand. As each person does this, a circle of golden energy is created. Draw the energy in through your left hand and arm and then feel and let it flow through you and on around the circle, out your right hand and so on. With each one in the group doing this, a greater force of energy is generated that also serves to include all participants equally. You may like to use your breath to aid the flow of energy, drawing it in from the left as you breathe in and directing it out from the right as you breathe out. This can also be viewed as breathing in circles, to link with the circle of the Full Moon.

Once clearly established, which you will feel through you, the circle can then be visualised by each person as rising and expanding above and beyond the circle of people and continue to do this until the room you are in is filled, or the space you are in feels enclosed in this radiating, golden light. This will serve to protect and cleanse whatever environment you are in and give you safe conditions to work in. It is a pleasant option here for one member of the group, perhaps a different member each Moon, to say aloud a few words asking for protection, guidance and safety. This is best done in your own simple, sincere words, spoken from intuition and inspiration of the moment.

This deals with the protection necessary before we begin. As we saw, we also have a need to regulate and be in control of the energy that is raised and emitted through the meditation. It is also necessary to ensure that when healing force and energies are sent out from the working group or circle, it is not originating in the individuals concerned, so sapping them of their own life force. This is all too commonplace amongst healers who continually give good and effective healing, to find that they are themselves continually ill, tired or run down. When giving out energy in this way it is necessary to ensure that what you are giving out comes not from you, but through you. This is a subtle but big difference. You are effectively a conductor for a current of force that is not your own.

For this reason I have given here an outline of a procedure that I call Grounding and Connecting. This process serves to ensure you are in a state of balance prior to opening yourself to the full light of the Moon. Ideally this should be performed before each and every meditation that you undertake and certainly should constitute the first section of your Full Moon Meditation. Another effect of Grounding and Connecting is that it will ensure that what you experience in your meditation, at any time it is performed, is not a flight of fancy or imagination.

Meditation is a subtle subject, where things rarely hit you between the eyes (though it may feel like this at times!). Instead the realisations come gently and sometimes like a fleeting glimpse of some truth you have longed struggled to know. Like dreams, they can present themselves to you and then be gone. We need to know then, that what is experienced is real and need a reliable means that we can trust will enable us to bring these back to our conscious minds.

Remember at this level of meditation, as with many others, you are working from and contacting the subconscious level of the mind. Again like dreams, when you are in that realm you may think that what you are working on will stay with you when you return. On returning from your meditation, or on waking from your dream, you may find that other things have entered your mind. Even the smallest thought can take you away from what you were thinking and the realisation, or the message of the dream, is lost.

If however, you dutifully perform your Grounding and Connecting prior to each meditation that you do, you will find that things will not slip awa,. like a wolf in the night, but you will return with them intact. This is because you are connected in essence with that which supports and gives you life, above and below. Once grounded and connected you are held as if in suspension between the worlds, safe in the arms of the Universe and your Mother Earth. When you then make a gradual return from them you are able to bring with you what you have learnt, instead of plummeting back to the waking world with the speed and subtlety of a stone falling from the sky.

Whilst it may seem like a complicated and lengthy procedure when explained on paper, with a little practice you will find that it can be performed within one or two minutes. The process includes much that is of great value and many people have found that Grounding and Connecting on a daily basis transforms their life. It can be taken as a meditation in itself and gives a wonderful feeling of calm and inner balance at its conclusion.

Grounding and Connecting can be viewed as a state of being as well as a meditative procedure. Being grounded is to be fully awake and aware of oneself and in control of one's faculties. Many people find this increasingly difficult in these times of pressure, from many different angles. The daily practice of grounding oneself, sending energy down into the Earth, can be a great help in establishing a firmer grip on reality and giving the ability to cope with all it throws at you.

In my work in Meditation and similar fields I have encountered many people who are clearly not grounded and many badly in need of it! Such people are the 'New Age' sweetness and light brigade, for whom every day brings a major advancement on their path and a great revelation. They cannot travel anywhere without a half-hundredweight of crystals secreted about their person or giving everyone they meet a "message from spirit". My message is to get grounded and to get real!

Spirituality is real and therefore can be found in the dirtiest of towns as well as the beautiful places of the world at any given time. The challenge is to know the reality of this while you are there and to live still according to your truth. This way you can be of service, not to the 'poor unfortunates' trapped with a drinking or smoking habit, but by example, leading a normal and healthy life in which you radiate these things to others. You become like a magnet to others and this is indeed what you are.

It is well known that the Earth's energies are magnetic and that in our hemisphere they head North. When in the process of Grounding you relax yourself, in whatever way is comfortable for you, you then become aware of yourself as more than just body, but of mind and Spirit and the energy or life force that constitutes these. This energy has a pulse and movement, that permeates your whole being - physical and energy bodies. Remembering again that energy follows thought, you then concentrate on your feet and on where you make a contact with the floor beneath you. This has the effect of sending this life force or energy down to your feet. You may feel as if your feet and legs have become very heavy, or warmer or that they are tingling.

These are all sensations brought about by the movement and flow of energy and are quite normal. You may not feel them, which is normal too!

From your feet think of sending your energy down into the Earth below you. Whether you are on the top floor of a tower block or lying in the Dead Sea, the Earth is below you. Imagine that your energy flows down in a stream to join with the body of the Earth. You may feel a pull downwards as the energy responds to your thoughts. Focus on your energy linking with the Earth. You may choose to colour the energy that you imagine or visualise in your mind's eye, brown or green to connect with the Earth. Imagine that it seeps down into the soil and blends with it. Soon it flows deeper down, into the very core of the Earth.

The Earth is a powerhouse of energy, more than able to support all life, in part magnetically. As we connect with the Earth in this way, the Earth's natural response is to send us back a stronger dose or flow of life force. Imagine then, the energy you send down mingling with the nutrients and minerals amongst the soil. Open yourself to become aware of the heartbeat of the Earth and its very essence. Let your own heartbeat merge with the Earths and soon you will begin to feel the Earth pumping its energy up into your being and body. Feel it rise like sap through you. It will permeate your body inside and out and will flow through every bone, muscle, vein, sinew, piece of tissue and fluid that is your body.

Feel a strength and vitality flowing through you and gain a sense of security from this. Open yourself from within and receive this energy and gift from the Earth - She will gladly give of her bounty in this way. You may feel a deepening of your awareness and feel for the Earth environmentally as a result of repeating this process, so perhaps I should warn you that you may find yourself peacefully protecting your local green space or sacred site from a new road, in which case - Congratulations! As the energy gains in strength and flow you simply allow it to continue its climb up over and in your body, pumped by the Earth and your own concentration. You can then turn your attention to the next stage in this process, that of Connecting. Connecting is really the same process, but in reverse, so above you.

Bring your point of attention gently and easily up to your head and to a place just a little above the centre of the top of your head. Here the energy centre or Chakra known as the Crown is housed. This is in part what allows you to receive life force and energy from the Sun and the Universe itself, that is above and all around you. By keeping your concentration and indeed your whole self in this place in your meditation, you serve to generate an energy flow to this area. This in turn stimulates the chakra, which responds and 'opens' or unfolds. This means that it expands and like the petals of the flower the chakras are often likened to, opens out.

In your meditation you can then open to receive the energy flow that is constantly being sent to you, to sustain and nurture life, from the Universe. Imagine this as coming from the farthest reaches of space, from the Sun and in the air around you. Feel it as a purifying and cleansing force, lighter and finer than the Earth energy. You could imagine this as a white light or perhaps the colour of violet, being the colour of the Crown Chakra, or wheel of energy, as this term means. As you keep your concentration fixed upon this process, which is vital in any meditation, you will feel this Universal life force flow down through your body and whole being.

Allow it to flow through and merge with every part of you. Feel it giving you healing and cleansing your system. It will also put you in touch with your inner and subtle senses, that are wakened and stimulated into conscious action, made possible by the link the flow of energy provides. Feel your intuition and your sense of inner knowing. This is what your intuition is - it is inner-tuition, teaching from within. You may also feel as if you have become much taller through this process and that your head has expanded. Again these are normal sensations that may or may not occur. The object is to have your feet firmly on the ground and your head in the stars. This is the meaning of Grounding and Connecting.

Once this flow of Universal energy has become established within you, you can allow it to continues its work, which is its natural inclination, This will naturally bring you to a point of balance that lies at the very centre of your being. This is the mid point between these two 'complementary opposite' energies. At this point you can experience the balance at the heart of yourself and indeed, the whole Universe. For you are now grounded and joined intrinsically to the Earth beneath your feet and to the Universe above and around you. At this place there is perfect rest and perfect calm. It is possible to remain in this place for the remainder of a meditation and gain much, in the way of experience as well as realisation. This gives you a wonderful feeling and a deeper peace than any you may have felt before.

For our purposes however, the aim is not a heady experience or only to gain peace within, essential though this is to the healthy person. We have a definite goal in mind through our meditation and it to this we must now turn. You may choose to leave a minute or so of silence in your group before continuing however, for the human mind cannot continually concentrate for too long a period. It is good practice then to leave gaps between naturally occurring sections of your Full Moon Meditation. These are indicated in the layout for the suggested meditations and provide a chance for the participants to rest and simply relax before continuing. This will also give each individual the very pleasant experience of the balance that lies at the heart of Grounding and Connecting.

In our journey we have reached the Moon and sojourned long upon its surface, exploring and learning. Now it is time to harvest the fruit of that learning and put it to some use. The Moon is full. Let the meditations begin.

11. FULL MOON MEDITATIONS

I have given here a suggested layout for your Full Moon Meditation. You will see that this is general and can be applied for each of the meditations through the year. I have set the meditation out in this manner deliberately, so that it requires a little work from you, in terms of reading the material to make yourself familiar with it, rather than just reading out a prepared script in the meditation. If you have to invest a little time, effort, emotion and therefore energy in preparing your Full Moon Meditation, it will be all the more effective when you do it. Remember, energy follows thought. if you are not prepared to do this, are you ready for Full Moon Meditation?

I have given some guidance notes for each of the principles and energies of the signs of the Zodiac. These can be incorporated into the meditation at the appropriate section, dependent on which sign the Sun is in. Names from various traditions and countries are given, which can also help to identify the particular nature of each Moon. These will overlap, since traditions vary their interpretation of each Moon, due in part to where they are in the world. The more familiar you become with this, the more effective your meditations will be. You can of course, discuss and decide on your own names for the Moon's, to describe its nature as you understand and work with it.

Of course more than just the meditation can be conducted at your Full Moon Celebration. Since ancient times the Full Moon's were a time of celebration, of the blessing of the Goddess and the appearance of maximum light in the darkness of night. People would gather by the light of the Moon to meet, on hilltops and sacred places and meet folk from their area to converse, pray, meditate, enact ritual, dance, drink and eat. There is nothing that say our present day gatherings must be a solemn and hushed affair. Sacred yes, but this can be acknowledged and celebrated in many ways. Use your imagination and invent your own ways to honour the Goddess.

Also given are the keynotes for each Moon, given to us by the Tibetan Master Djwahl Kuhl, writing through Alice Bailey once again. These can be used as Affirmations if you wish. Affirmations are statements of purpose or fact that determine a particular way or action. This acts rather like programming oneself, again following the 'energy follows thought' principle. Perhaps the whole group can say the words aloud, slowly and deliberately to allow time for the words to sink in. Alternatively they can be repeated silently within the mind, to provide more of an inner focus. These statements are meant for your own contemplation and meditation.

Also included are connections that the Moon has through the zodiac signs, with various parts of the body, taken again from the traditional and accepted astrological links. It is good and helpful to be especially aware of that part of the body at the time of the Full Moon for that sign, in this way using the Full Moon Meditations as a system for maintaining and improving overall health and well being. The ruling colour associated with the zodiacal signs are given and these can be incorporated in your celebrations, by way of decoration, cloths and candles used etc.

We now arrive at the layout for the Meditations. Please be aware that these are only suggestions, which you are free to experiment with and amend as you wish. There are several sections to each meditation and I recommend a pause of a few minutes or as long as seems appropriate for people to relax and rest. Any individual, no matter how expert at meditation (a state that does not exist!) cannot concentrate for too long with the degree of focus that is required for some parts of these meditations.

You will find that by allowing your participants to rest between each section the overall effect is more powerful. By letting your meditators come gently back to that place of balance between the Grounding and Connecting they will be allowed to rest from their concentration, physically shuffle if they wish, but not actually leave the meditative state of altered consciousness. If this does occur it is possible to lose the subtle awareness and the energy raised so far and the effect of the meditation is lost.

By working in waves of this kind the momentum is maintained and the power increases. It does so in such a manner as to be gradual, rather than blasting your poor sitters with the total force of the Full Moon from the beginning. Instead take your time and work through it gradually. You have five days to work in, so there is no rush!

Below then is the general outline for each of the meditations, which will need to blended with the information given for each of the separate Moon's.

OUTLINE FOR FULL MOON MEDITATION

1. If it is clear, and late enough (depending on the time of year) go outside and look at the Moon. Recognise it as the Goddess and allow yourself to bathe under her influence for a time, soaking up the rays and force. On the rare occasions in Britain when it is warm enough, the complete meditation can be performed outside.

2. EXPLANATION. Have one person (perhaps different each Moon) briefly outline the influences and energies for the Moon, as given in this chapter. Do not spend too long on

this as you do not wish to tire everyone's concentration before you begin. This does help to focus everyone's mind on the work however.

3. ATTUNEMENT. Form a circle, and perform the Attunement, as given in the previous chapter, to attune yourself to the sensitivity required and to instill the necessary protection.

4. GROUNDING AND CONNECTING. Perform the Grounding and Connecting procedure, also outlined in the previous chapter.

5. PAUSE

6. INVOCATION. In meditation, focus on the Crown Chakra and be aware of the source of light, full and round, high above you. Feel the influence of the Moon within and without. Imagine silver light from the Moon flowing down to the centre of the circle you are in. Work on keeping it there, building up in power and force. This requires concentration and may become uncomfortable, especially around your head. Keep your focus whatever - remember this is your work of service. Hold the energy, until you feel that the circle will burst.

Spend as much time on this as you feel is necessary.

7. DISTRIBUTION. Let the energy flow out from the circle, across the globe. Visualise the Earth in your mind's eye and see it bathed in the silver glow from the Moon, the light and energy flowing from your circle, or from within yourself if you are on your own. Focus on those

people, places and situations that are in most need at that time, for whatever reason. Here you can lend support to world leaders working for good, for healing, peace etc. To my mind there should be an emphasis here on your own local area, so that each group working across the globe (eventually!) is responsible for itself. 'Think globally, act locally'!

8. PAUSE.

9. REFLECTION. Turn inwards to yourself and have a time of silent reflection, for each individual. Consider the individual nature of that Moon, and absorb the energies coming from it within yourself. One person can remind the group what these are, from the notes following here. Focus on the part of the body that Moon is linked to, strengthening and healing it. Let yourself become attuned to what nature is doing. This will have its effect on your outer life as it becomes instinctively attuned to the cycle of the year.

10. AFFIRMATION. Repeat, aloud or silently, the keynote affirmations for that Moon, letting the words soak into your mind and reflecting on their meaning.

11. GROUND. Repeat the Grounding procedure (not the Connecting!) to Earth yourself after the meditation and return fully to the everyday world. Ensure that your return to your usual state of waking consciousness is attained before moving or standing up, lest you find yourself back on the floor quicker than expected! Stretch gently and return completely to where you are, adjusting your senses back to normal.

12. DISCUSSION. Spend a little time for each to voice their experiences as they wish. This is a valuable experience where much can be revealed, exchanged and given.

13. CELEBRATE! The inner celebration and effort is over and now is the time for outer sharing, communion and celebration. Share food and drink, perhaps asking each member to bring suitable items (Moon shaped cakes and red wine go well with the Full Moon). You can of course hold a communion of sacred food (ask the Goddess to bless it first) during the meditation. I would suggest after the Grounding at the end, as this will also help that process. Don't forget to pour an offering of a drop of wine and a few crumbs on the Earth for the Goddess.

There is much scope for individual interpretation in this suggested layout, which is as it should be. Do experiment and discover what works best for yourself and your group. This will all go to make your meditations more effective, for yourself and the rest of the world. Always remember that this is your 'prime directive'.

Outlined below then are the influences particular to each Moon. Remember that each Moon is determined by the sign of the Zodiac that the Sun is in at the time the Moon is full. There are therefore twelve different Moon's to each calender year, occasionally two occurring within the same sign. In terms of our work through the Meditations, this means that we will be producing the same energies and effects from the heavenly bodies. This seems to me to give us the opportunity to provide an increased concentration or dosage of those energies. The Goddess is turning to face and bless us with double the strength.

From the notes below the specific nature of each Moon can be determined, from the names, the affirmations as well as the characteristics of each zodiacal sign. Be aware of these as you Invoke the energies, for their nature differs drastically, just as the nature of those born under those signs differs. The celebration of the Moon is the celebration of individuality and togetherness! Of course these notes can be added to, for they are very basic only and any astrologers in your group can be of great use here, providing more insightful comments than my untrained mind can do.

I will begin the notes with the traditional beginning of the astrological year, when the Sun is in the sign of Aries. This is the time of year also when the major cycle of activity, as previously described, through the Moon's of Aries, Taurus and Gemini begins, which suits our purpose well.

ARIES MOON

MARCH 21ST - APRIL 19TH

NAMES: SPROUTING, EGG, SEED, EASTERN, PLANTERS, FISH, SPRING, DO NOTHING, DEEP WATER, ASHES, LITTLE FROGS CROAK, LEAF SPLIT, BIG WIND, NEW LIFE, WIND TOSSED, SAP, SCYTHE.

The Aries Full Moon occurs in the sign of the Ram, being symbolic of the creative impulse and the inception of spirit, thereby linking it with new beginnings. It is a time when the darkness of winter is gone and the light of summer arrives. Animals are emerging from their winter hibernation and we too can focus on coming into the light.

The beginning of the time of Aries falls on the day of the Spring Equinox, when day and night are in balance. From here on there are more hours of daylight than night time, so we have more of a solar than lunar influence affecting us.

Any new beginnings in our lives can be helped along and it is good to be aware of a new cycle of life beginning, as in the natural world. We can look to see where our potential lies and what we can bring to fruition in the coming months, like the seeds that can be planted now.

This can be a time of creativity, not least in a fertile sense, it being mating time for foxes, and arrival time for lambs coming into the world. Just as the cuckoo heralds spring now, so we can herald our own inner nature and begin to allow ourselves out into the big wide world, eager and ready to act.

All the new growth needs space to prosper and develop, and we can make use of the 'Big Winds' of this Moon, letting them blow our inner habits and outmoded ways away, left from the deep dark of our winter rest. Stand atop of a hill and let the wind blow through you, perhaps under the Moon. You may even feel an irresistible urge to howl!

In meditation examine your impulses and urges that stem from within, driven by the Aries energy. Allow yourself expression and assert what you intend. Be spontaneous and out working, in speech, thought and action. Ariens are forthright people, exerting strong self assurance. We must ensure we do not become rash, but follow our instinct to act and move ahead. It is good to be outdoors, usually where you will find Ariens. Arien rams are renowned for rushing in 'where angels fear to tread' and so it is good to be calm and still for a time too, being wary of the quickness to anger Ariens can display, as the fiery energies of the Sun take a rampant hold within.

PART OF BODY: Head, showing the need to be at the head of things.

COLOUR: Red

KEYNOTE: I come forth and from the plane of mind I rule.

TAURUS MOON -
APRIL 20TH - MAY 20TH

NAMES: MILK, MOTHERS, HARE, FLOWER, CORN PLANTING, CUCKOO, GRASS, FLOWER-SHOWER, PINK, BUDDING TREES, MILK BUCKET.

The Taurus Full Moon marks the high point in the year of spiritual activity, regarding the activity of the 'Masters', when as the legend told of in Alice Baileys books says, the Buddha and Christ align and meet "at a rather high altitude in the foothills of the Himalayan-Tibet ranges", when pilgrims and travellers gather to celebrate and give honour. Now we can meet and give honour in our own way.

This is a celebration of spring, the ancient festival of Beltain falling while the sun is in the sign of Taurus. The fertile rains fall in intermittent showers, blessing and causing the newly planted crops to grow. All is fresh and full of life. Everywhere flowers and trees blossom and animals and insects are at large again, scurrying and searching. Beltain is a time for purification by fire, which can be done symbolically (or literally, by jumping the flames) in the meditations, taking the fire within. This is a time of gathering and celebration of the 'merry month', so invoke joy and the spirit of family and friendship, together with fertility. It is important that all this joy and activity is earthed and used in some practical manner, by being expressed and shared. Taureans are apt to be restrained and passive.

Taureans can also be steadfast and determined, qualities which we draw on to strengthen our resolve for the coming summer months of hard work and activity. Steady progress is our watchword now, for there is a strong need for security, to ensure success. The spirit of togetherness can thus be seen to have many positive aspects. Nurture your strengths within this security and do not allow yourself to become stubborn, as Taureans can be. Instead change that stubbornness to determination and move forward. Look to see where your security comes from. Consider your need for and use of material resources, and try to be aware of the effects upon the Earth these things have. Allow your need for security to travel upwards to a higher source, that has its reflection and presence within your heart. This can give a peace that truly does 'surpass all understanding' (as well as personal trauma and emotion) and will never depart. You can allow its presence to fade and become distant if you wish, but that is your choice. The sense of peace will never go, the whispers will never die.

PART OF BODY: Neck and throat, as supportive of the head and higher senses and connection. Also Thyroid gland and ears.

COLOUR: Blue/green.

KEYNOTE: I see and when the eye is open all is light.

GEMINI MOON -
MAY 21ST - JUNE 20TH

NAMES: MILK & GAMES, PLANTING, WHITE LADY, FROGS RETURN, HONEY, ROSE, FLOWER, MAKING FAT, STRAWBERRY, HOT, SALMON FISHING, RIPENING STRAWBERRIES, CORN, STREAM.

This is the third in the series of Moon's of peak activity in the year. Now the energies are distributed and we allow the tension we have been building up to dissipate. There is an essential communication between our own inner spirit and those of all people the world over through this connection.

This communication is reflected in the sign of Gemini, whose main attributes and influences include self expression, being extroverted and communicative.

We can explore our own self expression and ask ourselves how truthful we are being, to ourselves and others. Geminians are adaptable and versatile, blending well with others. We can use these energies to allow ourselves to say things we need, to let out that which has been held within.

This is a time for balance, since it takes us to the centre of the year, the time of the Summer Solstice, when the sun stands still for a moment before continuing its journey. We too can pause for a time, for a moment's silent reflection amidst the heat and the activity. As the symbol for Gemini is the twins, this expresses the diversity and duality within each human soul, the inner male and female which we need to balance and unite.

Geminians are traditionally restless and adapt to change very well. This is a good time to bring about change in our lives, examining ourselves to see if we are ready for this. We can use the restlessness and the urge to travel we may feel, urged on by the long hours of daylight, to motivate us to change and adapt our lives more according to what we would wish. There is often a lack of interest in long-term plans, living for the moment. We can use the time of meditation to ensure we are in touch with our true emotions and direction.

There are tendencies to be over excitable now as well, Geminians feeling often that they have to avoid dullness at all costs. Time spent in meditation is therefore time well spent, giving some quiet and rest amongst the noise and glare of sunshine.

PART OF BODY: Shoulders and arms, as vehicles of expression and communication. Also respiratory and nervous systems.

COLOUR: Silver/Amber

KEYNOTE: I recognise my outer self and in the waning of that self, I grow and glow.

CANCER MOON -
JUNE 21ST - JULY 22ND

NAMES: MIDSUMMER, ROSE, SUNSHINE, STRAWBERRY, THUNDER, BUCK, MEAD, SUN HOUSE, RIPE, WHALE, BLACKBERRY.

The time of the Cancer Moon begins with the Summer Solstice celebration, when the Sun reaches its zenith. This is a natural time of celebration, as we have mentioned. This is a time when much work is done outside, taking advantage of the available light. We too can look out from within to see the effect of our actions, and see the results of what we planted in our lives some months ago. Are we yet ready to harvest those deeds or must we sit and wait patiently for them to ripen. Although written deliberately in agricultural language, these words and suggestions can also be taken literally for whatever you are doing in your life. Consider also the life of your group. Remembering that what happens within, happens without. Talk, communicate and be sensitive to all needs in the group, for those quiet ones may be saying more in their silence than those who talk loudest.

Sensitivity is a key issue to the crabs of Cancer. Like the crab they are often hard on the outside, seemingly able to handle anything and not given to large public displays of emotion. Underneath however, there is a soft side that needs nurturing and caring for and needs to feel loved as we all do.

Consider in your meditation if you are caring for yourself and those around you. Are you nurturing yourself along, to achieve the best you can and are you treating yourself kindly? Also ensure that you are not being over-sensitive in any area, as there is a great deal of protection that Cancerians employ to retain their security within.

Cancerians are renowned for not making a decision or taking action until they are sure of the outcome and result. In part this stems from an urge to protect and nourish themselves. In your meditation then, see the likely outcome of your current actions. Are you acting selfishly or are your actions leading to well being of body, mind and spirit?

Cancerians can have a tendency to cling to the past, so this is a good time to examine your life to see if there is any area in which you are living in the past, taking refuge perhaps from a more challenging future where more effort is required. Recognise that the Solstice time is one of subtle inner change in the cycle of nature and use those natural forces and energies to facilitate your own change, if you find these things difficult.

PART OF BODY: Breasts and stomach as the link with nurturing and security within. Also alimentary (nourishment) system.

COLOUR: Emerald.

KEYNOTE: I build a lighted house and therein dwell.

LEO MOON -
JULY 23RD - AUGUST 22ND

NAMES: COMPLETION, HEAT, FIELD POPPY, STRONG SUN, HARVEST, WHEAT WIND, CORN, RIPE BERRIES, GRAIN, WOODCUTTERS, STURGEON, WART, SUMMERTIME.

From the Names attributed to this Moon, we can see that all things are moving towards their harvest, the crops ripening to completion under the strong sun. This is a time not of lazing under the heat, but of working, hard and hot, in the long hours of daytime left, to gather all in before the first frosts come.

The Leo Moon then is a time of harvest, during which the ancient harvest festival of Lughnasadh is celebrated, with many ancient customs practised to ensure the spirit amongst the corn was not cut, but preserved. Now we can ensure that we are harvesting what we have brought to fruition in our selves and in our lives.

Be careful not to disregard the inner essence and spirit of what you have achieved and the motivation and joy it has brought you. Always look for progress and forward development, seeing that which lives on through your activities, like the spirit in the corn, which must be preserved and valued. Then it can be used again, calling on these deep inner resources, which the strength of the sun at this time can reach.

Leos can be unrelenting in pursuit of their goals and we must determinedly press on, though this may seem a time of things losing power and energy, like the sun begins to do by the end of August. We must draw now on the strength of the lion that is the symbol of Leo. This is not a physical strength necessarily, but an inner strength. In the Tarot card of this name, a lady is shown taming a lion by holding it in a certain position. This makes it feel accepted and recognised, for she knows and respects its power. So the strength we must use now is an inner one, that comes in part from recognising our potential for destruction and power, that can be used positively and negatively.

The lady and the lion of the Tarot card also represent the feminine and masculine respectively, the masculine here being identified with the power and physical force of this outer aspect of the personality. By balancing these forces within us we can begin to feel that we are at last taming the wolf, as the symbol for that which we fear. Now we can begin to understand the need to howl and to face that which is wild within us.

Leos are often fun-loving types, so this is a time when we can let ourselves go. Leos experience powerful feelings, that are sincere. These can be motivated from a desire to be at the centre of attention, so we should look within to see what the motivation in our own actions is. Often showy, Leos have almost a need to run things their way, so we should ensure we are not giving way to the temptation to be self centred and to remember our call to service at this time.

PART OF BODY: Heart, as an expression of strong feelings and the source of power, like the Sun. Also the back and spine.

COLOUR: Gold/yellow.

KEYNOTE: I am that and that I am.

VIRGO MOON -
AUGUST 23RD - SEPTEMBER 22ND

NAMES: HARVEST, HARVEST HOME, FRUIT, DYING GRASS, BARLEY, COOL, LEAF YELLOW, ALL RIPE, BIG FEAST, LITTLE WIND, SICKLE.

From the above Names we can see that this Moon has to do with the culmination of things. At this time of year the harvest is completed and a 'big feast' held. This is why the name of harvest is given to this Moon and not the previous one. There is little wind, as we see, and things turn cooler.

The leaves change colour and prepare for death. Yet it is in this death that the fertility of the natural world lies. As the leaves fall they are absorbed into the ground, along with the nutrients they have and the life force that the Earth will soon absorb from this sacrifice.

This is reflected in the symbol for the sign of Virgo, that of the virgin. She is traditionally depicted holding a sheaf or ear of wheat, to symbolise fertility and it is to this power that we can look to perform our work of service, by focussing on our connection with the Earth and our responsibility at this time to 'heal the wasteland'.

Virgoans are by nature generally critical yet practical people, with an urge to analyse and investigate. Their abilities to dismantle things in order to understand their workings is unique, the crux being whether they are able to replace the parts to make a workable whole! Usually the Virgoan will not settle until they have perfected their understanding in this way. This can easily turn itself into being over critical and pedantic, with oneself or others. They have a need to ensure maximum efficiency of their energies and also to be free from the influence and dependence on others.

These aspects can be used in your meditation, focussing upon your opinion of yourself, without judgment. Are you being overcritical, of yourself or others? Consider also what you perceive to be perfection in your life. This can be things you want, things you do, where you live and much more besides. How perfect are they and do you think you deserve better? Remember that anything is possible, but not everything is beneficial.

The time of this Moon brings us back to the time of balance between day and night, dark and light, when we reach the Autumn Equinox. We can again seek this balance within ourselves and in our lives. Look for a balance between the inner and outer aspects of your life, between thought and deed, between emotion and action. Offer the first fruits of the harmony and peace that comes from your balance to the Goddess, for it is truly she who provides all for all.

Look to finish projects begun before the summer now, for now is the time for approaching darkness, when all things turn inward. Just as there is balance between day and night there is balance between Sun and Moon. This is the time when the Sun begins to acknowledge the power of the Moon and we can feel this within ourselves during the meditations.

PART OF BODY: Abdominal region, intestines, spleen, central nervous system, as that which we can absorb and respond to.

COLOUR: Pale blue/Turquoise.

KEYNOTE: I am the mother and the child, I, God, I, matter, am.

LIBRA MOON -
SEPTEMBER 23RD - OCTOBER 22ND

NAMES: HUNTERS, LEAF-FALLING, DUCKS-FLY, BLOOD, CHANGING SEASON, DEER RUTTING, BASKET, CIDER BARREL.

We are now in the time of greater darkness than light, the more lunar than solar time, that marks the time spent within, looking inward and following guidance from there. It is also a time of letting go, leaving behind that which is no longer needed in our lives, that has become outmoded and needs to be discarded. All around there are signs of this in the natural world as the leaves fall, leaving the trees bare and barren. The bones of animals that have died rot and decay into the Earth now, and with this process we must recognise the need for this death and renewal process.

Mother Nature is gathering to herself stocks for the winter, to ensure the survival of as many of her children as possible. The berries that fall from trees now go to provide a time of plenty for many of the small animals of our woodland areas. We too can be gathering ourselves for inner strength, to see us safely through the dark winter months ahead.

Having with it the symbol of the scales, Libra is primarily concerned with balance and ensuring that all is in harmony. This has an echo of the Autumn Equinox, at which the time of this sign begins. From this balance, within and without, stems the impetus for progression. Librans are great peacemakers and we can look for peace within ourselves, also ensuring of course that we are at peace with who and what is in our lives at this time.

There is a love of beauty and justice present in the Libran that enables us to ensure that all in our lives is just, in thought and action. This is a time when we can assert to put right that which we truly feel is unjust, both in our personal lives, whether giving or receiving, as well as justice in other places of the world. We can send this 'vibration' of energy out to those places in need of some justice!

A fault of the Libran often is to be plagued by indecision. We should then use this time to see if we are procrastinating in any area and ensure that we are not delaying things in our minds. Uncompleted projects and ideas now are apt to be left until the return of spring, when we may have lost the drive and ambition we once had. The time for action is now.

This is also a time for selflessness, that blends well with our acts of service for this Moon. There is a strong romantic streak to the Libran and whilst this can obviously be a pleasant thing, it is as well to ensure that this romanticism does not override the purpose of service that is very serious.

PART OF BODY: Kidneys, as that which maintains harmony and eliminating what is unwanted.

COLOUR: Blues/greens.

KEYNOTE: I choose the way which leads between the two great lines of force.

SCORPIO MOON -
OCTOBER 23RD - NOVEMBER 21ST

NAMES: BEAVER, FROSTY, AUTUMN MOON, ALL GATHERED, STOMACH MOON, FREEZING, INITIATE, BLOOD AND BONFIRES, SNAIL SHELL.

We can see from the names of this Moon that we are now firmly in the grip of the cold weather and frosts. This is the time when the white of the Goddess begins to become more obvious, as the greenery of the summer God all but disappears. Now we can see the famous red robin singing to herald the onset of winter. We can see signs of the red of the blood of life on the holly plant, traditionally bound with ivy.

This Moon includes within it the time known as Samhain, usually called Halloween nowadays. This is a time when the old year dies and the new year is reborn, in Celtic terms. It is a time for gathering, in the sense that all that can be taken from the fields has now been stored for winter use and families and friends come together for celebration, bonfires being lit to guide them home and symbolic of the new life in their new year, as well as to persuade the Sun not to leave.

We can then light the fire within ourselves, the fires of light and love that we can now express to each other and indeed to our own selves, where it is perhaps most needed. Look for the seeds of new hope and life in the decay of the old.

Scorpio is the sign of the scorpion, indicative of the Scorpio nature of toughness and ruthlessness. These qualities can be of positive as well as negative use, if we channel them to a desire to serve and to heal. Scorpios often direct these energies inappropriately, in tender matters of the heart and we must take care to be gentle to ourselves. There is a basic energy and instinct for perseverance in the Scorpio nature that can be of great benefit, driving us forward, through our meditations, to what we strive to achieve.

As befits the time of year, the Scorpio is essentially introverted and passive. We can take these traits to ensure that we blend with the movements of Mother Nature as she too settles down and expresses her inner nature. This is a very personal and subtle time wherein each must really discover for themselves what is the nature of this time and how they can relate to it. This is a time then for silent reflection, to draw things out from the depths. Recognise those depths and allow the truth to surface in a positive light. This is a time when we go within and regenerate ourselves in our own private way.

PART OF BODY: Genitals, as the connection with the power of regeneration.

COLOUR: Scarlet, purple.

KEYNOTE: Warrior I am and from the battle I emerge triumphant.

SAGITTARIUS MOON -
NOVEMBER 22ND - DECEMBER 21ST

NAMES: LONG NIGHT, CHRISTMAS, CHRISTS, OAK, NIGHT, COLD MONTH, ASHES FIRE, TURNING, MIDDLE WINTER, BIG FREEZING, HUNTING.

In the midst of the obvious cold and winter time of the above names we meet the fiery sign of Sagittarius, offering us some warmth and passion to see us through the long nights. All is still and quiet at this time, when nature rests and recovers from the efforts she has made before. In this stillness and slumber, the year is quietly reborn, like many of the ancient sun gods, in a cave deep in the heart of the Mother Earth. This is the time of Yule, when for Christians the Christ was born.

At this time we can look for renewal and rebirth, of that hope that brings the promise of what is to come. There is an optimism in the Sagittarian personality that we can make good use of now, allowing the warmth of their fire to fuel us.

Sagittarians can be fickle, changing from one thing to another without warning and causing confusion to those who do not understand this process. We need to apply this understanding to ourselves, searching to see if this fickleness has a place in our own lives. Consider what motivation there is to continue you as you are and maximise these feelings.

The ability to exaggerate comes with many a Sagittarian personality, as they have a love for the dramatic, driven by their passion. Do look to see that you can see things as they truly are, for their real worth. Concentrate on long term plans for the coming year, and enjoy the Sagittarian urge to explore and seek out freedom, constantly heading towards the next horizon.

In the depths of winter now, dreams can be especially relevant, as we live in the abode of lunar rule. We have seen elsewhere the link between dreams and the Moon, with the subconscious mind. Let these images and visions speak to you as you wake gently. This time is suited to the pursuits of philosophy, law and religion, from whatever perspective.

The enthusiasm of the Sagittarian is another trait that can offer us much in these cold times. This driving force manifests in many ways and we can take these underlying energies within to keep us moving, lest we freeze! Do ensure also that you do not become prey to the insensitivity that Sagittarians can adopt.

PART OF BODY: Hips and thighs, as that which drives and controls direction.

COLOUR: Amber/Orange

KEYNOTE: I see the goal, I reach that goal and then I see another.

CAPRICORN MOON -
DECEMBER 22ND - JANUARY 19TH

NAMES: WHITE GODDESS, LONG NIGHT, COLD, LONG SNOWS, WINTER, WOLF, OLD, ICE, PLAY, KNIFE.

Now the time of 'long snows' is upon us, when these days we seem to become obsessed by the weather, panic gripping us at the first sight of snow. The tide has turned however and the days begin to become longer, noticeably so after a few days. We have passed the time of Yule, the wheel of the meaning of this word having turned and with it the impulse of nature begins to beat again, quiet yet and frail, but gaining in strength all the time.

As we begin to move through January the light strengthens and lengthens, even if it is aided by the reflection of the snowfall on the ground. The stores of winter are beginning to run low and we look to the waxing strength of the Sun to make new shoots appear soon. We need to dig deep within ourselves and draw on the strength we should have gained from the previous Moon. Let that fire burn and feed the Earth of this sign from beneath. Let the warmth melt the cold in your own heart and the frosts you present to the world will disappear too.

Capricorns are patient and persevering, traits which are in great demand if we are sensible and await the return of spring. This is not a time for outer action, but of inner strengthening, little by little. Capricorns have a disliking for hardship yet we must ensure we do not give way to greed or impatience, but make steady progress. The Capricorn is prudent however and plans coolly and efficiently, helping us in our natural tasks at this time of year. Mentally they are calculating, but can have tendencies to be severe, so we just ensure we are not making undue demand on ourselves, not only mentally but physically too.

This Moon brings with it a call for self discipline and organisation. The long and hazy months of summer may yet seem a long way off, but now is the time when we can get our inner house in order, ready and healthy for when the demands are made that can otherwise drain us. Capricorns are not given to displays of emotion, so this is a time for work on the inner levels.

PART OF BODY: Knees, as that which is able to bend and give way as the need arises.

COLOUR: Black/Violet.

KEYNOTE: Lost am I in light supernal, yet on that light I turn my back.

AQUARIUS MOON -
JANUARY 20TH - FEBRUARY 18TH

NAMES: SNOWFALL, EARTH RENEWAL, HUNGER, STORM, TRAPPERS, BUDDING TIME, ELDER, WIND, RUNNING SEASON, FRIGHTENED, PLOUGH.

We come at last to the time when the Earth renews itself and we can see the beginnings of the buds, sprouting their green shoots into the light. The long darkness of the winter is over and we begin to see that the light triumphs once again.

During the time of Aquarius we reach the ancient and beautiful festival of Imbolc, the time of cleansing and purification. Within, we can focus on cleansing out that which has now become outgrown as we discard the outer winter garments too, to beckon the return of the advancing spring. We need now to clear out from within that which is no longer pure, using this 'Cleansing Tide' to ensure we do not hold on to that which cannot now be of use.

This time of year has been known as the 'Hunger Gap' for the winter stores have all but gone and there is still time before the Earth can provide us with the food we need. This is a time for renewal and we can renew our commitment to serve and to give, of course to others but also to ourselves. We need to acknowledge our own needs, for health and optimism and determine to continue to provide these things.

The Aquarian nature comes to us now, bringing with it a spirit of friendliness and communication. This is a time for contact with others and for acting more spontaneously than before. Aquarians often break with tradition and are unconventional. We too can leave old traditions behind and instead allow the new energies coming in to us, for the new year as well as the new age, to affect and spur us on.

This is a time for individual talents to shine and we can look within to see where our talents lie. These things can be used for the good of all rather than for personal gain or greed. There is a strong intuitive feel now, and so we can allow communication to deepen and flow from this vital aspect of our nature.

The Aquarian has strong humanitarian urges and can put an intensity into what they believe. These characteristics and energies are of great use in our purpose of serving, and great advances can be made now as the typical Aquarian energy typifies the new age of humanity that we are beginning. Align yourself with these during this Moon and you will find it easier to adapt to the changes that are sweeping our world order and system.

PART OF BODY: Ankles, as that which turns and adapts.

COLOUR: White.

KEYNOTE: Water of life am I, poured forth for thirsty men.

PISCES MOON -
FEBRUARY 19TH - MARCH 20TH

NAME: LENTEN, CROW, SAP, FISH, WORM, CHASTE, SNOWBLIND, FLOWER TIME, BIG CLOUDS, EARTH CRACKS, PRIMROSE.

The names of this Moon take us through the sparseness and meagre times of the hunger gap at its beginning, with the Lenten Moon, to the blossoming of flowers and the rising of Sap. We finish this Moon's time, and our journey through the wheel of the year by returning to that time of balance at the Spring Equinox.

In our meditations then, we reach again for that balance, seeking out the return of our ability to bring out into the open that which we have kept buried or hidden. The sap of spring can flow through our bones and provide us with the impetus we need to move into action.

The Piscean energy is one of emotional sensitivity, compassionate and kind. These qualities can easily be adapted into service, as we have compassion for others in need at this time, across the globe. We must ensure that we do not become bogged down in the emotions, instead opening ourselves through our meditation, then closing again. To ensure our own safety and protection.

Pisceans have a tendency towards the creative and the mystical, higher side of life. These are qualities that again can be of use in our purpose. There can be an impracticability about the Piscean, and so we should ensure that our plans and goals are achievable in the targets we set.

The watery fluidity of the Piscean urge can assist us to move onwards, for as we reach the end of a year of activity through our Full Moon Meditations, we must look ever onwards and upwards. This does mean however, that the Piscean energy can make us impressionable, so the call for practicality must resound once more.

PART OF BODY: Feet, as that which moves and takes us forwards.

COLOUR: Pink/blue.

KEYNOTE: I leave my Father's home and turning back, I save.

This completes the cycle of energies presented to us year by year through the influence of the Sun, as reflected by the Moon. Please remember these are given as food for thought only and are very far from being complete. Add to these your own notes from books, ideas and realisations from your meditations.

It is important to realise too that although these cycles repeat themselves each year, there is always a difference in them. There is always progress to be made, always an impetus to move forwards. Build the image in your mind of a spiral, getting higher and higher, reuniting and connecting us with that which we came from. As we move through the years fully into the Aquarian Age, so our lives will change and adjust, to react positively to and absorb those energies that underlie our very reality which in turn shapes our future. Through this system of Meditation we can become inwardly attuned to this way of life, fulfil our requirement to serve and so aid the healing of the wasteland. Let this be your aim.

12. THE RITUAL WAY

The use of meditation is only one way in which the Full Moon can be celebrated and the energy radiated out to aid in healing the wasteland. There are many people, whose number is increasing, who realise that ritual can be used to raise a goodly amount of energy, for many purposes. It follows that we can adapt ritual for our purposes, to be performed by the group, as an alternative to the ritual.

I have therefore given below a suggested ritual which I hope does not offend anybody as it is not intended to belong to any one tradition, system of working or ancient family line passed down since Atlantean times! It is intended as a guideline only, so please read it as such.

You might like to begin by wearing white, to blend with the Moon. Perhaps silver would be more specific, but this will help you to feel the part whatever. The robes or clothes you wear could perhaps be decorated with colours appropriate to the Moon you are celebrating i.e. Aries Moon, red and so on. Appropriate incense can be burnt, to enhance the group's perception. There are many choices available for this, individual and group experimentation being the best guide. You may like to try frankincense (sparingly - it gives off billowing clouds of smoke!)

To set up a sacred and safe space in which to work, it is necessary to designate the area in some way, sealing off the outside world from where you are and calling up the forces to aid your working. The most effective way I have yet experienced to do this is to use the Elements of Earth, Air, Fire and Water, one at each of the directions. I have read often confusing and conflicting instructions as to which one to begin with, so I will simply start at the North in this case, being the storehouse of Earth's magnetic energy, which we are attempting to distribute.

You may like to have appropriately coloured candles for each Element (i.e. Earth, North, Green; Air, West, Yellow; Fire, South, Red; Water, West, Blue) or you may choose to have white candles to represent the Moon: the choice is yours.

Begin by facing the North and raising the candle in both hands. It is best to have words of your own to request the power of the Element to be present to protect and guide you. Something along the lines of "Great Guardian of Earth we request your presence in honour of this sacred time. Be with us" for the North. These can then be adapted for each Element quite easily, following the order above.)

As the circle is cast in this way, the ritualists can stand round its perimeter (inside!) and visualise a circle of golden light climbing ever higher. Suitable words can be said on its completion to indicate your intention and purpose, to those now present. Again choose your own, perhaps like these: "Let the blessed circle of the Lady of the Moon be honoured and adored by these your servants. We see your light in the starry sky and unite our senses with yours"

Other words can then be spoken, perhaps by each person in turn, to further raise the awareness and energy of the particular nature of that Moon. For instance these might be, for the Libra Moon: "We seek and invoke the balance that lies within the Sun and Moon. Let these forces move through us and guide us".

Each one in the group could then make a statement of personal action or intent for their life during that Moon, or perhaps simply gesture as they will, to honour the goddess and acknowledge this time.

Then comes the work of radiating the energy raised out, in service to humanity. Visualise, with specific intent, the silver globe of light, reflected from the Moon, around the circle, filling it completely. Focus on this, with each person sitting at its edge. See and feel it shimmering and humming with power. See the light from the Moon pouring down into it. At a given word or gesture from whoever is leading the ritual, then change, perhaps with arms raised, to allow the energy to be distributed. See the great force of this silver circle leaving in the form of a great fountain, rising up above the group, above the town or place that you are in and flowing above the whole globe, until you can visualise the entire Earth being surrounded and held by this light. This can be a powerful way of working, so please be careful and gentle until you are used to the force. Stop again at a given word or gesture, when the leader/priestess/priest feels the work has been done.

A cup of spring water can then be passed around each one in the group, by way of taking the blessing of the Moon within. This should have been exposed to the waxing light of the Moon before hand, and blessed or consecrated, again with your own suitable words ("Please bless this water" will do the job). Allow each person to take a mouthful, with due thanks to its source. Feel this water circulating round your system, cleansing and purifying it.

The circle can then be banished, reversing the process used to construct it. Appropriate words of thanks and acknowledgements should be used, as the candles are raised and then extinguished in each direction. "We give thanks for your strength and protection. Depart with love and blessing". Do this in reverse order to that used at the beginning of the ritual. Remember to pour any water left back to the Earth and ensure all participants are safely earthed, perhaps by celebrating now with a feast or shared meal, before letting them loose into the world again.

There is much scope here for adaptation by groups of many traditions and systems of working, as indeed it is intended to have. This is a guideline only and should not be used as a script.

Many other methods of working can be introduced into this working. Many groups like to include dancing as part of a celebration, or hands can be held around the group at certain points to symbolise the unity we have and feel especially at the time of the Full Moon. Use your imagination!

In my (limited) experience of ritual, I have discovered that those that work and feel best are those that have been worked at and interpreted for oneself, even if clumsy, inept and impractical at first. These things all work out with practice and experience and there is only one way to get those. The above is therefore included, not because this is a good Full Moon Ritual, but in the hope of stimulating interest and even better, helping those who have never tried a ritual before to discover this sacred and powerful way of celebrating our divine nature. Good luck!

13. AT BREAK OF DAY

The original idea of this book was to provide participants of my own group with some background notes to assist them in their chosen task of service through Full Moon Meditation. These soon grew to approximately one third the size of this manuscript. By 'chance' I came across the publishers who requested I increase the size of the notes to enable its publication.

At this stage, those beings on the levels with greater vision than our own took over. I had a dream that unleashed the wolf within me and one that really shook me at the time. Through subsequent meditation I realised that the wolf had come to me to guide the work I was doing, along with his mistress who seemingly never leaves his side. The connection of wolves and the Moon then came to me and I set about the process of writing this book, that would also be the process for me, of taming the wolf.

Now that work is finished and still I feel the wolf with me, I am glad to say. I feel that every word has been guided by him, even down to this last chapter, the instruction for which came to me during a particularly patient meditation class! I realised then that a strong attachment had been made between us and, as he came and slumped down beside me, I realised that his work was done. I had tamed my wolf.

I was soon corrected however, when in a subsequent meditation I realised that the work was only just beginning. Now with the power and identity of the wolf within me, I was able to unleash this and by reading the book, it is my hope that this same process has occurred within you. By adopting this system of Full Moon

Meditation you are able to awaken forces in your life that are as ancient as the hills, containing their primal and instinctive power that can shape the world as we need it to be. Opening yourself truly to the energy of the Moon is to open yourself to what you fear and what you can learn. You can gain in strength and wisdom and bring in to your life an appreciation of things beyond explanation. They need to be experienced for yourself.

Through writing this book I have discovered why wolves really howl at the Moon. It is in exhilaration, in pain and joy that comes from knowing we are beings everlasting, born of something great beyond our comprehension. Again, this cannot be explained, only experienced.

I will close then with an image that occurs as I write this chapter, that of wolves roaming the hills and wild places of Britain once more. These wolves are not to be feared however, for humanity has tamed the wolf, not by submission and might, but by wisdom and love. Within those wolves I can sense and see the spirit of each member of humanity that has tamed each wolf. As I close the book, I can hear the howls echoing around the hills, no longer eerie, but beautiful.

BIBLIOGRAPHY

Nigel Ashcroft Jackson - Call of the Horned Piper - Capall Bann, 1994
Alice Bailey - Esoteric Healing, Lucis Press Ltd., 1988
- Glamour, A World Problem, Lucis Press Ltd., 1988
- The Reappearance of the Christ, Lucis Press Ltd., 1984
William Bloom - Sacred Times, Findhorn Press, 1990
Joseph Epes Brown - Animals of the Soul, Element, 1992
Page Bryant - Aquarian Guide to Native American Mythology, Aquarian, 1991
Richard Carlyon - A Guide to the Gods, Heinemann, 1981
Tom Chetwynd - A Dictionary of Symbols, Paladin, 1982
J.C. Cooper - Symbolic & Mythological Animals, Aquarian, 1992
Arthur Cottrell - A Dictionary of World Mythology, O.U.P., 1991
Donna Cunningham - An Astrological Guide to Self Awareness, CRCS Publications, 1942
Nerys Dee - Your Dreams and What They Mean, Aquarian, 1984
Dolfyn - Shamanism, A Beginners Guide, Earthspirit Inc. 1989
Encyclopaedia of Mammals (The) - Ed. Dr. D. Macdonald, Allen & Unwin, 1984
J.G. Frazer - The Golden Bough, Macmillan, 1922
Robert Graves - The White Goddess, Faber and Faber, 1961
Miranda Gray - Beasts of Albion, Aquarian, 1994
Grzimeck's Animal Life Encyclopaedia, Vol. 12, Van Nostrand Reinhold, 1975
Mabinogion (The), Penguin Classics, 1976
Marian Green - The Elements of Natural Magic, Element, 1989
- A Witch Alone, Aquarian, 1991
- The Gentle Arts of Aquarian Magic, Aquarian, 1987
Rosemary Ellen Guiley - The Lunar Almanac, Piatkus, 1991

Murry Hope - Practical Atlantean Magic, Aquarian, 1991
- Practical Celtic Magic, Aquarian, 1987
- Essential Woman, Mandala, 1991
Janis Huntley - The Elements of Astrology, Element, 1990
Pete Jennings & Pete Sawyer - Pathworking, Capall Bann, 1993
Carl Jung - Man and his Symbols, Picador, 1964
Jon Klimo - Channelling, Aquarian, 1988
Jeff Mayo - Teach Yourself Astrology, Hodder & Stoughton, 1964
- The Planets and Human Behaviour, CRCS Publications, 1985
Kenneth Meadows - Earth Medicine, Element, 1989
Patrick Moore - Signpost to the Stars, George Philip Ltd., 1986
Francesca Naish - The Lunar Cycle - Prism Press, 1989
Naomi Ozaniec - Elements of the Egyptian Wisdom, Element, 1994
Revelation of Ramala (The), C.W. Daniel, 1978
Anne Ross - Pagan Celtic Britain, Sphere, 1974
Jamie Sams & David Carson - Medicine Cards, Bear & Co., 1988
Richard Stoneman - Greek Mythology, Aquarian, 1987

Index

Other Titles Published by Capall Bann

A selection of other titles published by Capall Bann. A detailed illustrated catalogue is available on request, SAE or International Postal Coupon appreciated. Titles are available from good bookshops and specialist outlets, or direct from Capall Bann, post free in the UK (send cheque or postal order).

Animals, Mind Body Spirit & Folklore

Angels and Goddesses - Celtic Christianity & Paganism by Michael Howard
Animal Magics by Gordon 'The Toad' Maclellan
Arthur - The Legend Unveiled by C Johnson & E Lung
Auguries and Omens - The Magical Lore of Birds by Yvonne Aburrow
Book of the Veil The by Peter Paddon
Call of the Horned Piper by Nigel Jackson
Cats' Company by Ann Walker
Celtic Lore & Druidic Ritual by Rhiannon Ryall
Compleat Vampyre - The Vampyre Shaman: Werewolves & Witchery by Nigel Jackson
Crystal Clear - A Guide to Quartz Crystal by Jennifer Dent
Earth Dance - A Year of Pagan Rituals by Jan Brodie

Earth Magic by Margaret McArthur
Enchanted Forest - The Magical Lore of Trees by Yvonne Aburrow
Healing Home by Jennifer Dent
In Search of Herne the Hunter by Eric Fitch
Inner Space Workbook - Developing Counselling & Magical Skills Through the Tarot
Living Tarot by Ann Walker
Magical Lore of Animals by Yvonne Aburrow
Magical Lore of Cats by Marion Davies

Magical Lore of Herbs by Marion Davies
Masks of Misrule - The Horned God & His Cult in Europe by Nigel Jackson
Mysteries of the Runes by Michael Howard
Oracle of Geomancy by Nigel Pennick
Patchwork of Magic by Julia Day
Pathworking - A Practical Book of Guided Meditations by Pete Jennings
Pickingill Papers - The Origins of Gardnerian Wicca by Michael Howard
Psychic Animals by Dennis Bardens
Psychic Self Defence - Real Solutions by Jan Brodie

Sacred Grove - The Mysteries of the Forest by Yvonne Aburrow
Sacred Geometry by Nigel Pennick
Sacred Lore of Horses The by Marion Davies
Sacred Ring - Pagan Origins British Folk Festivals & Customs by Michael Howard
Secret Places of the Goddess by Philip Heselton
Taming the Wolf - Full Moon Meditations by Steve Hounslow
West Country Wicca by Rhiannon Ryall
Wildwood King by Philip Kane
Witches of Oz The by Matthew & Julia Phillips

Womens Studies

Menopausal Woman on the Run by Jaki da Costa

Environmental Education

Talking to the Earth by Gordon Maclellan

Capall Bann is owned and run by people actively involved in many of the areas in which we publish. Our list is expanding rapidly so do contact us for details on the latest releases. We guarantee our mailing list will never be released to other companies or organisations.

Capall Bann Publishing, Freshfields, Chieveley, Berks, RG16 8TF.